To Listen is to Love

The Simple Path to Joy in All Your Relationships

LIZ SCOTT

Illustrations by Becky Hawkins

NEWSCOTT

"Beautifully simple yet deeply profound. Let this book gently wash over you as you read it. Then read it again. And again. Each time you'll find something new."

Jessica Shipp
Former Community Connector

To Listen is to Love is a sparkling diamond of a book, written from the heart with a wonderful generosity of spirit. Drawing on her years of experience as a coach, Liz shares examples from her own practice and her book is packed with practical wisdom on how to listen to your own natural resilience and wellbeing."

Belinda Seaward
Horsemanship for Health

"In this wonderful book Liz talks to us about our True Nature and helps us to reconnect with what we truly are at our core: peace, love and wisdom."

Russell Pearson
Deputy Head

"There is so much to commend in this beautifully written, clearly articulated, short book. I hope you enjoy being wrapped in its warmth, wisdom and compassion as much as I did."

Caroline Brewer

To my dear husband Stu.
Thanks for your constant love, support
and encouragement.

CONTENTS

Please Pass This Book On!

This book is meant to be written in, carried around and passed on (rather than sitting on the shelf after being read). With this wish in mind, dear reader, I have left you lots of space here to write a note before sharing.

Enjoy

A Message from Liz

Hello and welcome.

'To Listen is to Love' is a book that is all about taking the fear out of being human. You don't need to feel burdened with anxiety, worry and doubt— that isn't what life is all about.

Life is about connection, love and the joy of being alive. Life is about exploring what's inspiring and fun, and also tapping into the peace-of-mind that is always in reach.

Life is full of creative possibilities.

Being human is a gift, it's a chance to see the deep beauty in the simplicity of life, and it's about understanding the power behind listening.

As you read this book, you'll see that when you strip away the fears and insecurities, life has a natural ease.

What would it be like to realise that you're deeply OK? What would it be like to know that those you love are rock-solid and resilient at their very core?

Read this book and discover how listening to yourself and others is the key that will open up a whole new experience of life for you, and show you possibilities that may not have been visible to you before.

Once you've read it, don't put it on your bookshelf. This book doesn't belong to anyone, its purpose is to be lent and passed on. Write in the margins and highlight your favourite bits. You'll know it's done its work if the pages are dog-eared and tatty.

This book is not a manual, or a 'how to', rather it's a guide to help you to navigate life's journey. It will have the greatest impact if you read it lightly, with an open heart and not with your intellect.

This book is not a book about becoming a better person, it's here to help you see that you are, at the soul of your being, the very person you've been striving to become.

It's time to stop striving. The mental noise that has held you back does not define who you are.

You'll discover that you are much more than you think you are.

As you start to listen out for your inner, authentic beauty, then you will also start to listen out for that beauty in others.

When you listen to yourself deeply you will begin to feel all that is possible for you. That's when you will experience what it is to be truly free.

I hope you discover, as I am discovering, the rich possibilities behind listening. It's so good to welcome you as a fellow-explorer on this journey.

Enjoy!

Introduction

"I know the answer," I said to myself. It was an answer that had been eluding me for days. It suddenly appeared from nowhere. The answer was to the question: "If you could change anything from your life, what would it be?"

I was out on the moors of Dartmoor, walking the dog with my brain in neutral when, 'pop' just like that, the answer arrived.

I'd been with my mum a couple of days earlier and she'd asked if there was anything I would have done differently in my life. As I sat with her, drinking a coffee and mulling the question I couldn't think of anything I'd change. Even life's horrid experiences, had taught me something and my life had turned out in a way that I liked. I was content, happy and fulfilled. Nothing needed to change ... yet I had a niggle. *Was that absolutely true?*

Up on Dartmoor that niggle was resolved, it was like an itch that had been scratched. *Yes, there was something I would change in my life.* The answer lay with a woman, let me call her Beth, who I had seen 20 years previously whilst training as a counsellor.

As a trainee counsellor I was fresh, eager and fully engaged in my work. I felt sure that the answers to my distressed clients lay in counselling models and theories.

Beth was in her 60s and had experienced sexual and physical abuse as a child, and domestic violence as an adult. When she came to counselling, she was living alone and living a half-life. She was haunted by her past; she was scared of her future and she was convinced that she was forever broken. In her mind, her traumatic past meant she could never be truly happy, and she would forever lack resilience.

As I listened to Beth tell me of her past, I too believed she must be broken - who could survive such a past? It seemed that I needed to build her resilience and confidence.

Beth enjoyed talking, she enjoyed the safety of the counselling. I tried everything I'd been taught, and I felt sure she would go away feeling better.

I used every theory and model I'd learned. One week we were on the floor creating a timeline, the next she was switching chairs talking to herself. I explained the drama triangle and Maslow's hierarchy of human needs. I had a small amount of knowledge of CBT and Transactional Analysis, and I used it all. I was a keen counsellor, but a rookie and I wanted to help my client as best as I could.

Beth eventually left counselling because she was moving to a new house. When she went, I realised I hadn't really helped her at all. She didn't seem more resilient and she still had low self-esteem. Nothing much had changed for her. She continued to drag her past around in a sack of bitter memories and her future would forever be dampened by the experiences of her life. I felt like a failure; it seemed that I wasn't very good at counselling.

If only I could see Beth again now. If I could change anything from my life, then returning and working with Beth would be the one thing I would do. Our time together would be so different.

If I could go back to that counselling room, I'd tell Beth something fundamentally true about life. I would want her to understand that:

• She wasn't broken (she just had some uncomfortable, habitual memories that kept creeping up on her).

- The very things she thought she lacked were the very things she was actually made of (resilience, wellbeing and confidence).

Beth wasn't broken, she just believed her thoughts. Her thoughts were so convincing and so compelling that she didn't question what they told her.

I wish I could have helped her see beyond her thinking and pointed her towards the ever-present space of resilience within. I wish I could have helped Beth realise her capacity for a fulfilled life, regardless of her past.

I think this shadowy memory of Beth is one of the drivers behind our Wellbeing Listener Programmes.

When my husband Stu and I started the Wellbeing Listener project, it was at the beginning of lockdown in 2020. It was a frightening and unsettling time and we wanted to give people a lifeline, to let them know that below the fear and alarm, they were still OK.

In the first year we engaged with two hundred people. Our simple message sparked a tiny movement and since then we've collaborated with community groups and started projects within our local town of Ivybridge. I'm privileged to see the lives of people transform as they begin to realise their True Nature. That's why I'm writing this book. I feel drawn to share this understanding with as many people as possible. If you'd like to join our Wellbeing Listener Tribe, then check out what we're up to at the back of the book in the section: 'How to Become a Wellbeing Listener'.

The start of this Wellbeing Listener story really began with Beth. Twenty years ago, after counselling her, I began a restless journey reading self-help books, going on courses and training in different psychological modalities. I knew there were big gaps in my counselling knowledge that needed to be filled. It was exhausting.

It was only when I came across the Three Principles (3Ps) or the 'Inside-Out' understanding, thanks to a chance conversation with a friend, that my agitated search ended. A slower, more reflective and richer journey began.

The 3Ps seemed to signal that I had come home, the answer was closer than I'd ever imagined, it was right within me all the time (if you'd like to know more about the 3Ps you can read the 'What are the 3Ps?' section at the back of this book).

We found the Inside-Out understanding so beneficial that over the years we've adapted our courses around it. We eventually started a Social Enterprise and closed our coaching business.

After all of this time I've been unlearning everything that I thought I knew.

The Inside-Out understanding has changed my life. It will change yours too.

Your life is not meant to be busy, frenetic and running at full pelt. You're not meant to be trying to control your thinking or build resilience or improve self-esteem. It is much simpler. It is this simplicity that we weave into our work today.

As my husband Stu and I engage in our community work around wellbeing my mind often goes back to Beth. What we teach our Wellbeing Listeners is the very thing I wish I could go back in time and tell her.

The message we share is straightforward and intuitive. We help people see the capacity for listening; listening helps unlock the natural built-in wellbeing of humanity.

Life is not as complicated as you think it is.

Your natural settled state is a state of gratitude, joy and peace-of-mind; this is true for all humans. As you see this in yourself then you'll discover a new depth to all relationships in your life.

Wellbeing Listening is a bridge for that sense of connection. Listening is a catalyst to help unlock wellness and mental health in whole communities.

Stu and I are curious: *What happens when a whole community experiences the power of being connected to one another?*

During the course of this book you'll follow a path that is similar to mine. You'll start to listen to your intuitive guidance system, your Inner Compass. You'll also realise how the noise of incessant thinking can derail you if you don't understand it.

You may also find yourself 'unlearning' and letting go.

This book will explore the power of listening. The starting place is to listen to yourself. You first need to deeply 'know-in-your-bones' that your True Nature is one of clarity, love and compassion. When you listen to yourself and when you listen for the wellbeing of others, then you are able to navigate life with more ease. It is like finding the 'off switch' in your busy head. You'll discover a simpler, quieter life that feels nourishing.

It's a good idea to allow time for light reflection as you read this book. At the end of each chapter you're encouraged to consider a particular topic. There's no need to write anything down, just give yourself five minutes to stare into space and roll the idea around in your mind as you would a boiled sweet in your mouth.

The book follows the journey I took with the Inside-Out understanding. It is the same journey I take our Wellbeing Listeners on when they attend our Foundation Programme.

When I came across the Inside-Out understanding it challenged some of the assumptions I had about the world. I thought the world could make me feel anxious, I thought certain situations were inherently stressful, I believed that people were broken, I was certain that resilience needed to be taught.

Through this book, we'll walk through each step together, chapter by chapter.

Chapters 1-3 show how these assumptions are wrong. The first three chapters point to two alternative and consistent truths about humans. The first truth is that you experience the world through thought and your thoughts are ever-changing. The second truth is that at your core, your True Nature is resilience, creativity and wisdom - you can't be broken.

Chapters 4-5 focus on listening. It starts with listening to yourself. When you realise you are not broken then you can't help but listen to others in a completely different way. You're able to see through the scare-stories that you, and others, tell themselves. When you see the deeper essence of connection, then you'll discover the power of natural healing in action. When you listen like this, you'll see how listening is the nourishing, loving foundation to all relationships.

Chapter 6 is an invitation to learn more. *To Listen is To Love* is like paddling at the edge of a warm, enticing pool. Chapter 6 is an invitation to dive in more deeply, to discover that there is a life-long enriching journey ahead. This is the start of learning more about your True Self. As you see that you are more than you think you are, you'll see the potential for the whole world to change. Wellbeing Listening is an opportunity for the world to listen, to love and to discover the natural joy within all relationships. You'll be drawn to listen to others and to touch that space of connection within.

There are many stories in this book. Whilst some details might have been changed to maintain anonymity, these are the stories of real people and their real lives. Each chapter has a simple and everyday story of Wellbeing Listening in

Action. Many of these stories are of every-day situations in the lives of ordinary people. You'll see how joy returns to relationships when you understand how to listen to others.

Wellbeing Listening is portable, practical and intuitive.

My hope is that you will offer Wellbeing Listening as a gift to those that you love and to strangers you meet. My hope is that Wellbeing Listening becomes your default way of interacting and connecting in your family and community.

But above all, my hope is that you will learn to truly listen to yourself.

TO LISTEN IS TO LOVE

Chapter 1

A Whole New Way
of Seeing Life

"Look deep inside your soul; this is where you will find the answer."
Sydney Banks *

The Power of Listening You Already Possess

Wellbeing Listeners aren't professional therapists; they don't analyse your circumstances or childhood.

Wellbeing Listeners are like you and me. They love their friends and family, and they want to support them.

Wellbeing Listeners aren't trying to make things better; they aren't trying to fix people.

Wellbeing Listeners know something about life. They know that everyone is OK at the level of soul; they know that the human experience has its ups and downs (and there's nothing to fix).

Wellbeing Listeners intuitively understand that listening is an act of love and healing.

Wellbeing Listeners are rock-solid listeners in their communities; they want to help others reconnect to their True Nature. Your True Nature is that feeling of ease, joy and lightness; it's when you have access to resilience, humour and peace.

This book will support you on your Wellbeing Listener Journey. If you've been on the Wellbeing Listener Foundation Programme, then you will recognise some of the stories. If

---

* The Missing Link. Published by International Human Relations Consultants

you are reading about Wellbeing Listening for the first time, then you will be reminded of two very simple things:

1. Resilience and wellbeing are built into your system.
2. Your moods and thoughts can temporarily cover your wellbeing, but your wellbeing cannot be damaged.

If you haven't been on the Foundation Programme, then this book is still for you. It's a chance for you to reconnect to your own intuitive powerhouse. As a listener you'll help others see through their anxiety to the freedom and peace on the other side.

Wellbeing Listeners are people who have big hearts and who realise there's more to life than the endless hamster wheel of trying and doing.

Wellbeing Listeners are willing to see through the confusion of insecure thinking. They see beyond unsettled thinking to the deeper, powerful energy of True Nature.

Read this book with an open heart and be aware that the way you think your mind works might not be true.

Let's start by looking at how your moods can quite literally change the way you experience the world. We call it 'Red Thinking' and 'Green Thinking' …. and it starts with a dirty cup.

Would You Divorce Over a Dirty Cup?

One day I walked into the kitchen and saw a dirty cup on the kitchen work surface. The kitchen was clean, the dishwasher was empty, and this cup was perched just above the dishwasher door. It was my husband's coffee cup.

In a split second my mind exploded, 'How dare he!'

A firework display of annoyance erupted inside me and an internal indignant voice started ranting in my head:

"He's so lazy. Doesn't he realise that I do all the cooking? And come to think of it I also get the groceries – oh, and I'm forever tidying up and vacuuming. All he had to do was to put one mug in the dishwasher and he couldn't do that."

As one thought was overtaken by another my anger became so great, I began contemplating whether our relationship was worth the effort. 'Maybe it's time for divorce.'

I went from 'dirty coffee cup' to 'divorce' in a nano-second.

In that moment I felt a combination of being under-valued, overwhelmed, duped and unloved; my relationship was in tatters and my life was a mess – and all because of a coffee cup.

Or was it all because of a dirty coffee cup?

On another day I walk into the kitchen and see a dirty cup on the kitchen work surface. I internally chuckle at my husband's forgetfulness then I put the cup in the dishwasher and get on with my day.

I share the coffee-cup story to illustrate a fundamental misunderstanding we have about how the world actually works. We're brought up in a culture that tells us that people and events can make us feel a certain way.

But that's completely wrong.

Other people can't 'make' you feel anything, it's impossible.

As the coffee cup story shows, the dirty cup (or my husband) hasn't made me feel a certain way.

How do I know that?

If the cup had the power to make me feel something, I would have felt the same way on both occasions he left out the cup. However I reacted very differently to the coffee cup on different days. On one day I felt unloved and I wanted a divorce, on another day I just popped it in the dishwasher.

What If No One Can 'Make' You Feel Anything?

If the coffee cup and my husband can't make me feel angry, frustrated or annoyed – then what is going on?

Let's return to the dirty coffee cup.

Imagine that you have the ability to see, with ultra-laser vision, the mood I am in when I first see the cup. With your

ultra-laser vision you see that my mood is coloured red.

In other words, I'm (metaphorically) seeing the world through a lens of Red Thinking.

It is as if I am wearing glasses that are tinged red.

This Red Thinking lens magnifies and exaggerates my experience.

In Red Thinking I see a world that is frustrating, annoying, unfair and overwhelming. In Red Thinking my mind is revved up and busy, in Red Thinking the cup looks massive, in Red Thinking the world is scary and overwhelming, in Red Thinking it looks like my husband doesn't love me.

In Red Thinking I experience a world full of insecurity and fear.

It's not surprising, when the world looks fearful and scary that I'm inclined to blame others and lash out.

What about on the second day I see a dirty cup?

Let's continue with our ultra-laser vision and see what's happening with my state-of-mind on that day.

With our ability to see through to my mood, what do we see?

On this day my mood is metaphorically 'green'.

I am in Green Thinking.

My mind is settled, and my thinking is calm. On this day I see things as they are and it makes sense to put the coffee cup in the dishwasher and get on with my day.

If you believe the world has the power to make you feel a certain way then you spend a lot of time and energy trying to change people, circumstances and your thoughts.

This is an exhausting place from which to experience life.

If on the other hand you realise that the world changes according to your mood and thinking (in other words the colour of your thinking), then you'll start to understand how things really work.

In Red Thinking you see the world as unfair or overwhelming or frustrating or frightening or scary or guilt-ridden or …… (fill in the gap).

When you are in Red Thinking it is like walking on uneven ground.

In Green Thinking you see the world as it is and you are on firm ground.

Do You Need to Learn to Think More Positively?

The most common question we are asked is: "How do I change my thinking from Red to Green?"

It's an understandable question because so many people love tools, techniques and strategies.

If something is broken do you love to fix it? If there is a problem, do you find it fun to find a solution? You're not alone.

We're raised in a culture that loves to apply intellect to working things out.

I spent 15 years looking for tools and strategies to fix myself and change my thinking. My bookshelf was so full of self-help books that I had to pile them up on the floor.

Five years ago I cleared away my books and gave them away.

I realised that trying to 'fix' and 'change' myself and

others was exhausting and never-ending. Rather than FIX I realised the power of UNDERSTANDING.

I hope you're not disappointed but there aren't any tools or techniques in this book.

Red Thinking and Green Thinking aren't good or bad or right or wrong.

They just are.

It's much more useful to UNDERSTAND how your thinking works, rather than try to change it.

You can't control your thinking. It does its own thing.

It's more helpful to see thinking like the clouds in the sky. Your moods and thoughts are forever shifting and changing shape – but like the clouds they are made from the same stuff.

- The cloud shaped like a face – is made from water vapour.
- The dark cloud with a silver lining – is made from water vapour.
- The wispy high clouds – they're made from water vapour.
- When you walk in a mist – that's water vapour too.

Your moods, like the clouds, might take a different shape – but they're all the same stuff – they're all made of thought.

- Guilt is made from thought.
- Anger is made from thought.
- Excitement is made from thought.
- Frustration is made from thought.
- Happiness is made from thought.
- Gratitude is made from thought.

It's pointless trying to answer the question, 'How do I change my thinking from Red to Green'?

You might as well ask the following questions:

"How can I get a dog to miaow instead of bark?"
OR
"How can I get this apple tree to grow bananas?"
OR
"How can I get the rain to stop?"
OR
"How can I change the tide from high to low?"

You can't change any of these things – but you can understand them.

No Tool, Tip or Technique Can Beat the Simple Truth

UNDERSTANDING is where the real power lies.

You can understand that the nature of a dog is to bark – the nature of a cat is to miaow. You can see that apple trees grow apples, and the rain will cease in time.

Once you understand the nature of things then you stop trying to change how they are; you instead align yourself with how they work.

When you understand the nature of the tide then you know there is no point trying to change the tide from low to high. The tide changes in its own time.

If you understand how the tide comes in and out (and you understand the rhythm of tides) then you will align yourself with how the tides work. If you want to row your boat down an estuary with an outgoing tide, then you wait for the tide to go out.

You can't make the tide change any quicker than it's going to change.

There will be times when you can't wait for the tide to change – you need to get rowing. If you row your boat down an estuary and you're against the tide, then you know it'll be hard work. The tide just does its thing – that is the nature of tides. There's nothing personal about them.

It's the same with our thoughts, feelings and moods.

When I UNDERSTAND how my moods work then I know that:

- When I feel overwhelmed – my whole world appears overwhelming.
- When I feel insecure – my whole world appears frightening.
- When I feel frustrated – my whole world is unsatisfying.
- When I feel unloved – the whole world seems against me.
- When I feel settled – I deal with whatever is in front of me as best as I can.

The world I experience will change according to my mood.

My moods shift and change like the clouds and as they do I experience a rainbow-colour of feelings.

My moods are not personal, they are no more 'me' than the clothes I wear. They come, they go, they shift, and they change.

That is the nature of being human.

You are designed to experience all moods, thoughts and feelings – in the same way that you are designed to see different colours, to smell different scents and to hear different sounds.

The colour red is not better than the colour green. The smell of grass is not better than the smell of smoke. The sound of a dog barking is not better than the miaow of a cat. The colours, smells and sounds are just information.

It's helpful to smell smoke, I'm able to detect if there is a fire. It's good to hear a dog barking, it might warn me that it's going to bite; it's useful seeing the colour red, that means I know when to stop my car at traffic lights.

What Are Your Feelings Really Telling You?

It is helpful to see your feelings as information. Your feelings are doing a great job of letting you know how you're experiencing the world. They're letting you know what to trust and what not to trust.

Sometimes I look at a coffee cup and I feel unloved and I want a divorce and other times I look at a coffee cup and I feel resourceful and put it in the dishwasher.

My feelings let me know if I'm settled (in Green Thinking) or unsettled (in Red Thinking).

My feelings let me know whether I'm aligned with my True Nature or whether I'm lost in a world of thought.

Your feelings are like the warning lights on the dashboard of a car.

They are giving you information about how revved up your thinking is. If your thoughts are revved up, you'll experience a world that is unsettling. If your thoughts are settled you'll find yourself able to navigate more easily.

When thinking is unsettled and revved up – it's letting you know that you're seeing the world in a distorted way.

There's nothing to do.

When you feel unsettled the dashboard of your feelings is alerting you to be cautious.

You don't need to fix the feeling. Like the weather it will change on its own, the trick is to not add any more agitation into the mix.

Seeing Through the Fairground Mirrors in Your Head

The more curious you become about your own thoughts, feelings and emotions, the less you'll be caught up in them. It won't matter which emotion you're experiencing because you'll start to notice your feelings instead of getting lost in them.

There is nothing personal about your mood-state, sometimes you're in Green Thinking and sometimes you're in Red Thinking.

When you see your moods like a weather-system, then you'll realise they'll pass on through; they aren't going to hang around.

Understanding is the key.

As you understand the nature of moods you'll naturally adapt your behaviour.

For me, when I'm in Red Thinking I tread cautiously. I know not to trust the way I'm seeing the world at that moment.

When I'm in Red Thinking I wait for my thinking to settle before making difficult decisions or before I engage in important conversations.

Have you ever been at a fairground and walked around those wobbly, misshapen mirrors? They are designed to make you look super tall, short or fat or wavy.

When you look at yourself in a fairground mirror, you know that the image looking back at you is distorted.

The fairground mirrors are another way of understanding what happens in Red Thinking.

In Red Thinking everything you experience is distorted. It is not a true reflection of what is actually happening.

Once you understand what is going on, then you tend not to trust the world you're experiencing when you feel unsettled. It is the equivalent of not trusting the mirrors.

It's really helpful to know this.

The natural progression, once you've started to understand this in yourself, is to understand how Red and Green Thinking plays out in others.

You'll naturally feel more compassion for others when they are immersed in Red Thinking because you understand.

You realise how frightening it feels to experience insecure thinking. You will naturally make allowances for their outbursts and behaviours, because you understand that they are temporarily experiencing an insecure world.

As a Wellbeing Listener, understanding the nature of Red and Green Thinking will help you listen with compassion. Compassion will naturally arise in understanding what is happening for the person you are with.

Summary

- Wellbeing Listeners aren't fixers or busy-bodies. They are people with big hearts who want to learn to connect with and truly hear others.

- You create your experience of the world through your thoughts and the world changes according to your mood, there is no 'objective' reality.

- The metaphor of Red and Green Thinking helps us see that the same situation (like a dirty cup) can look very different on different days.

- It's good to know what colour thinking you are in because that helps you to understand how clearly you are experiencing the world at any one time.

- All moods are made of thought, whether they overwhelm, whether they create anxiety, excitement, curiosity or frustration or whether they create a sense of gratitude.

- It's hard work learning tools, techniques and strategies. They often fail when you most need them (in the thick of Red Thinking).

- Understanding your psychological system is powerful; it consistently works the same way.

- Your feelings give you good information. They let you know whether you are in touch with your wellbeing, or whether you are lost in insecure thinking.

- When you are lost in your thinking you are on uneven ground, when you are in touch with your wellbeing you are rooted and steady.

FAQs

Does that mean I should let people get away with bad behaviour if they are lost in Red Thinking?

No, we don't suggest that by understanding Red and Green thinking it excuses bad or inappropriate behaviour.

What you'll start to notice is that you don't take things so personally because you understand why someone's behaviour is erratic.

You'll also find that you have more compassion for those experiencing Red Thinking.

Have you ever noticed that it is such a relief to be on the receiving end of someone who understands Red and Green Thinking?

Take the domestic example of the coffee cup.

If I were to respond to my husband when I was lost in Red Thinking, then it's likely I would say things that I would later regret.

The good news is that my husband understands Red and Green thinking. He knows that when I'm in Red Thinking I am not in touch with my True Self, so he doesn't take things personally.

He understands that I might be curt or offish and he has compassion for me in these circumstances. It means that arguments don't spiral, because we both understand Red Thinking.

We both make allowances for each other and we both look beyond the Red Thinking to the True Nature that is ever present in the other person.

In just understanding Red and Green Thinking we are able to listen for wellbeing in ourselves and others.

In Action: The Wise Grandmother

Following the first Wellbeing Listener session Jane was with her two grandchildren. The youngest one had 'a meltdown'. The older sibling was becoming a bit distressed at his brother's upset.

Jane was able to share in a loud voice (so that the younger child could hear) that there was nothing to worry about.

She said that the younger child was like a wave crashing against the shore with his emotions and soon these emotions would naturally pass, there was nothing to become unduly worried about.

The two grandchildren soon settled down and re-engaged with playing; the meltdown passed as quickly as it arrived. Jane was grateful that she understood the nature of her grandson's mood-storm.

She hadn't been worried; she didn't try to rescue him, and she didn't feel the need to stop him from crying. Jane knew to allow the storm to pass, to be a loving presence and to show the children that there's no need to be fearful of intense emotions.

Your Turn

Have you noticed how you react very differently to the same situation on different days? Do you have your own coffee cup moments with family, friends and colleagues? On one day you are frustrated and on another day you are calm? There's nothing to fix or change, but it's good to notice how this happens to all of us.

P.S.

Instead of trying to fix your world, friends, family and thinking - take time to tune in and notice the weather-system of your moods and thoughts as they pass through. Your moods and thoughts always change. What is your mood-weather-system right now? Noticing is key.

Chapter 2

You're Free to Enjoy Your Life

"This being human is a guest house.
Every morning a new arrival.

A joy, a depression, a meanness,
some momentary awareness comes
as an unexpected visitor.

Welcome and entertain them all!
Even if they're a crowd of sorrows,
who violently sweep your house
empty of its furniture,
still, treat each guest honourably.
He may be clearing you out
for some new delight.

The dark thought, the shame, the malice,
meet them at the door laughing and invite them in.

Be grateful for whoever comes,
because each has been sent
as a guide from beyond."

Rumi *

You're Not Scared of Life; You're Scared of Your Thinking

On our Wellbeing Listener Introduction webinar I tell the story of Buzz. He's our labradoodle and he loves to snooze beside me when I'm working at home.

---

* From 'Rumi Selected Poems', translated Coleman Banks. Published by Penguin.

Buzz sleeps peacefully until the postman arrives. Then this slumbering, happy, contented dog leaps into a frenzied ball of barking. He goes from peaceful to agitated in a nano-second.

Every day Buzz rushes to the door barking wildly and every day, once the letters drop on the mat, he shakes himself off, returns to my office and falls back to sleep.

For many years I watched this behaviour with curiosity. Why was he doing this? I couldn't understand why, every day, he would waste so much energy over the postman. Surely Buzz should realise that there was nothing to be worried about.

I spoke to my friend, a pet psychologist and asked her why Buzz went through this unnecessary daily rigmarole, why didn't he just keep sleeping?

"Does the postman ever come into the house?" she asked, 'No,' I responded. "That's why it's so mystifying. What's going on?"

"Well, that's your answer," she said.

She went on to explain that in Buzz's world he believes that the reason the postman never comes in the house is because of his barking. In Buzz's world barking at the postman makes complete sense. He's protecting everyone from a frightening experience.

Buzz misunderstands the nature of the postman. He thinks it's only down to his bravery that the postman stays out of the house.

Buzz wastes an extraordinary amount of mental and physical energy in this behaviour.

This story of Buzz has helped me understand many of my clients. People often come to me in agitation and worry. They too seem to think that worry and agitation are necessary to prevent things happening in the future. Like Buzz, they don't realise that they're worrying unnecessarily.

It's perfectly natural to sometimes feel anxiety and worry, let's face it we're human.

This excessive thinking can become debilitating when we add more worry and fear and judgement on top of the original worry. When you understand this kind of thinking it no longer has the same kind of hold on you.

You Are Naturally Content, Clear and Calm

Your psychological default setting is a bit like the settled Buzz when he is happy and content and lying down. Your default setting is one of peace and clarity and calm, and this is when you experience Green Thinking.

In this default setting you are in touch with the creative energy of life itself. In this default setting you are able to truly experience the joy and mystery and wonder of what it is to be human. In this default setting you find yourself falling into the present moment.

When I fall into the present moment I am full of gratitude at the extraordinary privilege of being alive and being human. When I am in the present moment life feels good.

This default setting might temporarily become clouded over by a weather-storm of thoughts and feelings. That's perfectly natural. We're human. It's good when you remember that your moods and thoughts are just passing through. Thoughts and feelings are natural and they can never damage or disrupt who you are at the core of your being.

When Buzz feels a twinge of anxiety at the sound of the postman approaching, that's useful information. He's on alert.

It's the same with you.

As insecure thoughts and feelings pass through you, that's good information. You need feelings to alert you to potential hazards. However, when you misread these feelings and start to layer on more and more thinking, anxiety and worry, then you (like Buzz) are wasting an incredible amount of energy over something that will never happen.

In my work I often come across people who are mentally exhausted. One of the most common reasons for this mental exhaustion is because people misread and misunderstand what's happening with their thoughts and feelings.

When you experience Red Thinking you can overreact

and try to rid yourself of those uncomfortable feelings. In your urgency to get rid of those feelings you inadvertently make them worse. It is like trying to put out a fire, but rather than damping the fire with water, you are pouring on petrol instead. You are mistakenly whipping up your thinking, rather than letting it settle.

In this book we want you to consider that Red Thinking (whether this is a feeling of sadness, guilt, worry or insecurity) is part of the human experience. You don't need to get rid of these feelings. It's much more helpful to understand the nature of thoughts and feelings and to see how natural they are.

Life as a Piece of Music

Have you ever seen an orchestra strike up?

When the conductor raises the baton, the orchestra with its violins, clarinets, cellos, oboes and percussion, starts to play.

The musicians are all playing different notes (and different instruments) but there is harmony. The whole sound contributes to the richness of the experience.

Being human is like being a piece of orchestral music.

Sometimes the music soars to the high notes, the flutes are then in their element.

Sometimes it's low, a time for the tubas.

Sometimes there is a loud beating of the drums, here the percussionist takes centre stage.

There are times the music sounds happy and sometimes it sounds sad.

There are times when music is quiet, sometimes it is loud.

Sometimes it is fast and sometimes it is slow.

A piece of music played on the same note, without any variation, would be dull. However, an orchestra in full flow creates a fluid sound and the music comes alive. It is a rich, varied and nourishing experience.

What if your life were like a piece of music?

What if you are designed to experience a vast range of 'sounds' that ultimately contribute to you being human? These sounds are like the different emotions and moods you feel. Like the instruments in the orchestra, these feelings are all necessary for the full human experience.

Being human requires you to feel every single emotion. There's no need to suppress or feel guilty or self-judge your feelings. Unresisted feelings pass through in time. The trouble begins when you start to fight or quash a feeling or emotion.

When you stand in the humanness of welcoming all emotions, that's when you appreciate the uniqueness of the music.

You don't need to resist some emotions, any more than you need to resist some musical notes over others.

When you allow the music to flow through you feel freedom. This sense of freedom is very different from the restrictive feeling of trying to control.

The Problem with Trying to Be Happy All the Time

For many years I tried to control my life.

It seemed to me that in order to be happy I needed the right job, the right husband, the right fitness level, the right diet and the right amount of money in my bank account.

I tried hard by setting goals, reading books and keeping to a strict regime of self-improvement.

Whenever my happiness dipped, I saw my efforts as a failure. I needed to try harder, read a new book or go on a new course. I might feel fleeting happiness, but lasting happiness was always just out of reach. I often felt guilty.

This guilt extended to my family. I began to feel responsible for my family's happiness. When I trained as a counsellor (and then a coach) it wasn't just me and my family that needed to stay happy. I began to believe I was responsible for my clients' happiness too.

Imagine all the guilt I felt. It was a heavy burden taking responsibility for the happiness of me, my family and my clients. If anyone wasn't happy then it was on me. I spent a lot of time feeling guilty and not good enough.

It was such a relief to realise I'd got it wrong.

It was such a relief to see that I'd been trying too hard.

Being human is about experiencing the whole range of emotions, it's not about being happy all the time.

When I realised I didn't need to be happy all of the time, then I also saw that I wasn't responsible for the happiness of others. What a relief to realise that the happiness of my parents, siblings, husband, clients and friends was not something I needed to fix.

There is incredible freedom in understanding this.

Have you noticed I've just used that word 'understanding' again? When you understand the ups and downs and the capacity for us as humans to experience a wide range of emotions, then you don't feel so compelled to control your thinking, or to control the people in your life.

In the previous chapter we looked at Red and Green Thinking and compared your moods to the colours you see. Your eyes are designed to see a multitude of hues and shades. It is the same with your emotions. You are designed to experience a full range of emotions. You don't need to resist emotions like sadness, judgement, insecurity or anxiety.

I remember a teacher's eager feedback during some training.

The teacher said she bumped into a young lad who was feeling low. He had argued with his mum before coming to school and was finding his studies hard.

Usually, she'd try to boost the student's confidence with some positive talk but something stopped her.

"I suddenly remembered us learning about the range of emotions we experience," she said. "I explained to him that we all have ups and downs. I told him that I have my off days too. I said there was nothing to worry about, it is completely normal."

The teacher then described how the young lad seemed to visibly relax with relief. "I knew there was nothing wrong with him and he seemed so relieved to realise this too," she said.

This very simple interaction is a perfect example of Wellbeing Listening in action. The student was having a bad day and that was OK, there was nothing wrong with him and he didn't need fixing.

The Wiggly Line of Life and Your Built-in Capacity to Enjoy It

During the first Wellbeing Listener Session I draw a wiggly line; it looks a bit like a roller-coaster going up and down. This wiggly line represents the natural ups and downs that we all have as part of the human experience.

No-one feels happy or confident all of the time.

Everyone has good and bad days. You have different emotions, thoughts and feelings from hour-to-hour and minute-to-minute.

Your feelings and thoughts are like the weather and the weather is constantly changing.

Today as I look out of my window, a grey autumn storm has blown in and the rain is lashing against the

window. The storm is a weather system passing through. It is not personal, it might stay for a day, or several days or it might blow away within the hour.

Your emotions are a bit like the weather.

Sometimes your emotions are wild and unsettled; sometimes they are warm and sunny. Like the weather, your emotions naturally shift and change, they are not designed to hang around.

When you understand your moods are like the weather then you wait for the storm to pass by.

The more you become curious about these passing thought-storms, the less debilitating they are.

Here's how one of our Wellbeing Listeners described it:

"My biggest fear genuinely doesn't exist any longer. Don't misunderstand this... I still have moments of self-doubt, worry and anxiety much the same as every other person but I no longer engage with it. I acknowledge how I am feeling then wait and watch as it evaporates!"

One of the greatest gifts you can give someone as a Wellbeing Listener is to help them realise that it is perfectly OK to feel the whole range of human emotions. It's natural to feel insecure, happy, confident, sad, guilty, overwhelmed, frustrated and angry.

Your feelings let you know about the weather passing through your mind. Your feelings do not tell you about who you truly are. Realising this can be a huge relief. Your feelings aren't telling you how worthy you are, or how incompetent you are; you can sit back and allow them to move through you, like the guests in Rumi's poem.

As a Wellbeing Listener you'll begin to feel compassion for others. Compassion naturally arises when you understand the fluctuations of being human.

When you understand Red and Green Thinking then it's easy to see that someone's behaviour is a display of their mood or thinking in the moment. You don't take moods personally.

Does Your Imagination Put Fear-Spells on You?

We all see the world through a lens of thought. Your whole experience of life is created through the powerful medium of thought. You create a world, via the data from your senses,

and this world comes alive through thought.

Imagination is another name for the creative energy of thought. Imagination is like a magician; it can create a world that doesn't exist, and you believe it is true.

For Buzz, his imagination creates a world where the postman might come into the house and attack us. It isn't the postman that is frightening our dog, it is Buzz's own imagination that is frightening him.

It is exhausting to try and control the world created by your imagination, you're not designed to do that. When you see through your exhausting imagination you taste mental freedom.

During the winter months, when the nights draw in, I often find myself walking the dog in the dark. When a bright moon lights the sky, I love walking up the lane behind my house and on to the moors. The skies are big, the stars are clear and the reflection of the moon on the stream is enchanting.

On some nights when I walk up the lane, my mind is sharp and grounded. I feel free, energised and grateful. On other nights when I walk up the lane my imagination starts to play up. That's when I jump at shadows, or my mind starts to imagine that a lion might have escaped and is waiting to pounce.

On these nights, my heart pounds and I am on alert.

On these nights I imagine what it is like to be mauled by a lion, what the newspapers will write about my death and how upset my family will be.

On a walk up the lane, adrenalin pumps through me, everything feels frightening.

Even though I know there is no lion, that I won't be mauled and there's nothing hiding in the hedges, even though I know all of this, my imagination creates a frightening world, and it looks real.

The next morning when I walk up the same lane it's hard to believe my fears of the previous night. That's when I laugh at the stupidity of feeling scared. When I see through the web of fear created by my imagination, that's when I know I'm back on solid ground, that's when I'm back in my default setting.

Your imagination can trap you by creating frightening worlds and scenarios that you believe to be true. Can you recall a time when your imagination did this to you?

When I see through my Red Thinking and see how my imagination has been scaring me, I often laugh. It is funny to see how I've been scaring myself.

During our training course, one woman started to tell us a fearful story about her son's future. She was worrying that he wasn't working hard enough at school, she was fearful that he wouldn't get a job, she was anxious that he would never be happy.

At some point during the day, she suddenly realised that she wasn't worrying about her son, she was worrying about the stories her imagination had created. It was these imagined scenarios, and not her son's future, that frightened her.

From that point onwards she couldn't stop laughing, she'd been scaring herself and when she saw through it, she found it funny. She still cared about her son, she still wanted the best for him, but from a place of Green Thinking, she realised she didn't need to try to control his life, she just needed to be connected, love him and be there for him.

You're Not at the Mercy of Life's Craziness

Do you have any control over what you feel?

For many years I tried to control my emotions. I genuinely believed there was a way for me to feel better if only I found the right formula, tool or technique.

I see things very differently now.

I can see that my thoughts, moods and feelings are not who I truly am. They shift and change and move. Anything that shifts and changes is temporary, it can't be who I am at my core.

We all have the capacity of focused attention. You have the capacity to put your attention either on the fears and anxieties of life, or in the settled space of awareness within.

When you place your attention on the storms of life and

on your unsettled thinking, then you find yourselves lost in a world of fear.

When you place your attention on the awareness within, when you notice there is a calm, settled space within, then you find yourselves in touch with the creative energy of life itself.

You don't have agency over which thoughts erupt in your mind, you do however have the capacity to redirect your awareness away from these fearful thoughts and instead to seek out that steady, constant space within.

When you find yourself in touch with this space then you find you are no longer at the mercy of thoughts, feelings, moods and circumstances. When you are in touch with this space within, you are able to navigate whatever life throws at you.

We are going to talk about this settled space in detail in Chapter 3. At the moment I want you to be alert to the fact that there is more to you than being at the mercy of the wild storms of life.

Let's return to the orchestra, do you remember we looked at it earlier? We used the metaphor of the orchestra to show that in the same way an orchestra has a vast range of instruments, so you experience a whole range of different feelings, thoughts and moods. In the same way an orchestra plays an array of music, so you have a range of moods and feelings through which you experience the world.

There are no tools, techniques or strategies in this book. When we talk about Red and Green Thinking this is just a first step towards realising that the world works very differently than we are taught. There is much more to this book (and the Wellbeing Listener Course) than Red and Green Thinking.

There is much more for you to see.

You Are More Than You Think You Are

Have you ever watched a river? There is a beautiful Dartmoor river that gushes through our local town, speeding over rocks and boulders.

If you watch the river you will notice that the water seems to be constantly flowing. However, look more closely and you'll also see that in places the river swirls around in an eddy. These small pools of water aren't moving forward, they are spinning around and momentarily stuck.

That's what can happen if you start to become intrigued by thinking, feelings and moods. You too can become caught in an eddy.

How do you know if you're caught in an eddy?

It usually happens like this:

- Red and Green Thinking is a revelation.
- You realise you don't need to control your thinking and it will pass.
- You find relationships are suddenly more easeful.
- It's all going swimmingly until …
- Then you start to notice that some people still seem to annoy you.
- You wonder if you've got this Red and Green Thinking right.
- You wonder how to make it 'work' again!

This is all perfectly normal. Many people have this experience.

This is the equivalent of swirling around in an eddy.

Red and Green Thinking is just a step along the way of a nourishing life-long journey.

Let's return to our orchestra again. It can be so tempting to become lost in the music, to be fascinated by the musicians playing. This book is not here to help you become lost in the music; this book is here to encourage you to take a further step. A step within.

You are not the orchestra playing the music.

There is a more fundamental intelligence and energy behind life.

You are the energy from which the music is being created.

You are more than the music, you are more than your thinking, you are more than your moods.

You are more than you think you are.

Shall we take the next step into this vast energy of potential? Are you ready to take a peek at who you truly are?

In the next chapter we take a step within and we look at the metaphor of the Inner Diamond.

It's time to leave the river eddy of Red and Green Thinking and to continue this exquisite journey; allow the momentum of the water to pull you along.

When you're ready, it's time to move onto the next chapter.

Summary

- You are designed to experience a full range of emotions. Highs, lows, ups and downs. Think of your emotions like an orchestra. Every single instrument represents an emotion, and each emotion is needed for the full human experience.

- It's a relief to realise you can't control your emotions. You aren't able to be happy all the time. You are not responsible for the happiness of others. As a Wellbeing Listener it's good to remind others of this too.

- It's OK to have ups and downs. Humans are constantly shifting through the weather-pattern of their emotions. As a Wellbeing Listener it's good to let others know that there's nothing wrong with any emotion they might feel.

- Your imagination can create frightening scenarios that look and feel real. If you don't understand what is happening you can feel trapped through fear and worry.

- It's quite common to feel relief at seeing the nature of Red and Green Thinking. You're likely to feel more easeful and relaxed. It's also quite common to fall back into old habits and behaviours. Keep noticing what is going on for you. There isn't a 'right' way.

- There is a settled space of awareness within that is constant regardless of the shifting storms of your moods. Place your attention on this space, this is where you will start to get a sense of who you truly are. You are more than you think you are.

FAQs

How Can I Have More Green Thinking?

It's really tempting to see that Green Thinking is more desirable than Red Thinking and that you need to experience more Green than Red Thinking.

The work of our Social Enterprise (The Inner Compass Guide CIC) is not a 'How To'; there are no strategies and techniques. As a Wellbeing Listener we don't want you to strive for more Green Thinking. That's not what this training is about.

If you ask the question 'How can I move from Red Thinking to Green Thinking?' you are asking an impossible question. It's like going to the estuary and wondering how to change the high tide to a low tide. Or it's like looking at the weather and saying, how can I stop the rain and get the sun out again?

As a Wellbeing Listener we want you to UNDERSTAND the nature of moods and emotions. As you better understand them you'll find yourself aligning yourself with the way the psychological system works. Once you see through your moods you'll discover how these moods can shift into feelings of ease and lightness.

We often use a snow-globe to illustrate the nature of agitated thinking. When a snow-globe is shaken, the glitter represents your unsettled thinking. You know that the glitter will settle if it is left alone. You don't need to 'do' anything to make it settle, if you don't agitate the snow-globe further then it will settle.

When you listen for wellbeing (we talk more about wellbeing in future chapters) then this is the equivalent of allowing the snow-globe to settle. Listening is the catalyst to provide the space for fresh thinking to emerge. You don't need to apply a technique; you just need to become accustomed to listening for your built-in intuitive wisdom. We call this space your 'Inner Compass'. Your Inner Compass is pointing you back towards that space that resides within.

The first step of being a Wellbeing Listener is to become aware of your internal space of clarity and calm. There is something within that feels like the 'observer' of your weather-system of moods.

Listen out for that space within you.

Notice that regardless of the storms or sunshine of moods, there is a part of you, a deeper part of you that is the witness of it all.

Rather than trying to control Green and Red Thinking, notice what kind of thinking is filtering your world at any one time.

As soon as you 'notice' your thinking, you've already started the process of allowing your thinking to settle.

In other words, you're letting the weather-system pass on through.

The more you become curious about the settled space of awareness that is ever-present within you, the less agitated you become with Red Thinking.

In Action: Taking the Hassle Out of The Morning Rush

Here's an example from a mum who started to understand how it was her moods that were creating her feeling of annoyance and not her children. She describes it in her words:

"One morning we were late for school. As usual, Jack was ready, but Sarah was faffing. I felt myself getting more and more annoyed at Sarah's seeming inability to get out of the door. I asked gently several times and felt the anger and frustration rise. Then I snapped and shouted at her to hurry up.

As soon as I'd snapped, I realised what I'd done and apologised to Sarah. Jack (age four) made a joke out of it and made us all laugh. We got to school on time, we enjoyed our walk there and we all had a good feeling inside.

Before, I would have snapped, then remained annoyed, probably a lot of the way to school, lecturing Sarah along the way about why it's important to be ready on time. I would have then spent a lot of mental energy feeling frustrated about how annoying Sarah is in the mornings, mixed with guilt that I'd snapped at her and that I even find her annoying at all. Eventually I would forget about it and know that I love her no matter what.

I see clearly the enormous amount of mental energy this requires compared to the scenario I found myself in when we laughed and joked. The outcome is the same (love and forgiveness) but the journey to get there is so very different."

Your Turn

Be curious about the different spectrum of moods you feel – don't take them personally – be the observer, watch them as if you were watching the weather outside your window.

P.S.

You'll often find yourself mesmerised by your thoughts. It's tempting to try to change thoughts and feelings. However, there is a part of you that is untouched by the soap-opera of your personal world. Seek out that part of you, that is where true nourishment lies.

Chapter 3

You Are Unbreakable

*"All we are is peace, love and wisdom and the power to create the
illusion that we're not."*

Jack Pransky *

It's Impossible for Two People to Have the Exact Same Experience

Did you know that every single person in the world is having a completely different experience, even if they're witnessing the same thing?

Have you ever heard a radio commentary of a football game? I remember listening to a local radio commentator who loved Plymouth Argyle. When I listened to him commentating on the game he was passionate about his team scoring goals and he was dejected when they were losing. I could feel the emotional highs and lows translating through his words.

If I listened to the same game, but instead tuned into the commentator who supported the opposition, then it would sound like I was listening to a completely different game. There would still be highs and lows, but they would be transposed. When one commentator was cheering because of a goal the other would be downhearted and sad.

What would happen if I (someone who is not particularly interested in football) watched that same game with the sound turned down. In that instance I would just

---

* Quoted on Jack Pransky's website https://insideoutunderstanding.com

witness two teams of footballers running around a pitch. Some would score goals, some would save goals .... I would have no particular emotional involvement with what was going on.

What Radio Station is Playing in Your Head?

You (like everyone else) live with a commentary running through your own head. The constant commentary may sound like:

- Passing judgement.
- Remembering things from the past.
- Worrying about the future.
- Questioning others or yourself.
- Condemning others or yourself.
- Feeling victimised or vindicated.
- Telling yourself if you're 'winning' or 'losing'.

This commentary, in your head, is never-ending and so normalised that you don't notice it. As it babbles on and on it can be exhausting

In this chapter you will start to see through this exhausting internal commentary.

You don't need to try to change the commentary or quieten it or make it more positive. Instead of fighting to change the commentary, you'll find it easier to explore your built-in resilience and wellbeing; we call this your Inner Diamond.

Your Inner Diamond

When you touch base with your Inner Diamond then you will start to trust your intuitive wisdom.

Beyond your moods, thoughts, beliefs and internal chatter you'll discover a deeper presence and knowing.

This presence and knowing is witnessing the chatter of your mind and it is witnessing the state of your mood.

This deeper knowing is never influenced or changed by your mood. It is a neutral observer. From the perspective of this neutral observer, life is less frightening to navigate.

TO LISTEN IS TO LOVE

It really does something to shift your awareness to this space of knowing-presence within you.

I bet you were taught that you need to get busy if you want resilience and wellbeing. In this book we want you to see that resilience and wellbeing are naturally at the core of who you truly are.

You Are Already Resilient So Don't Waste Time Chasing What You Are

The Wellbeing Listener Programme is based on the Inside-Out understanding, some people know this as the Three Principles (3Ps). I will share more about the 3Ps at the end of the book.

Before coming across the Inside-Out understanding I thought resilience was a bit like a muscle. You needed to build it by going through tough challenges. The more tough challenges in your life, the more able you were to be resilient in the future.

It was important to build that resilience muscle. Bounce-back ability was something that needed to be worked on.

I see resilience very differently now.

I don't see that it is something that needs work and attention. Instead, I see that resilience is always present, regardless of the circumstances you're presented with.

Once, whilst I was speaking to a headteacher about resilience she was very challenged by the idea that all her children had resilience. She told me the story of a young child, from a troubled family, who would often arrive at school distressed. This young girl would run to the library and hug a teddy bear and refuse to speak to anyone. Then after 10 minutes or so, she would start to speak to her teachers and go into class. "That's not resilience," said the head teacher. "We need to build her resilience."

As I listened to the story I was touched to the core. To me this was a beautiful illustration of resilience in action.

The child, who had a very challenging home life, was understandably insecure when she arrived at school. Despite her home life and despite her mental distress she had the presence of mind to go to a very safe space (the library) and to not engage with anyone (she wasn't ready to) and to cuddle a teddy bear (she found this soothing) and she did all of this intuitively.

At some level she was listening to her resilience (that quieter voice of knowing) and allowing her wellbeing to emerge again. Then once she felt settled and was in touch with her wellbeing, she reached out to the adults she trusted and went back into the class to engage in learning.

I pointed out all of these things to the headteacher and she paused thoughtfully.

Then in an awe-struck voice she said, "I'd never seen it like that before. The children that I didn't think were resilient are the most resilient of all. They could teach us about resilience."

I couldn't agree with her more, but it seems that most of us have been misled about what resilience is and where it comes from.

In this chapter we'll be sharing a very simple and life-affirming truth about resilience.

When you start to understand the truth about resilience for yourself this makes the biggest difference of all.

Resilience is built into your system and it is constantly showing you the way. It is always helping you to rebalance and to return to your default setting of wellbeing. Let's take a look at this default setting, we call it the Inner Diamond

Tuning into Your Inner Diamond

In all our Wellbeing Listener programmes, whether it is with leaders, educators, charity workers, volunteers or children, we explore something we call the Inner Diamond.

The Inner Diamond is the metaphor we share when we talk about the default setting of wellbeing and resilience.

It is a simple metaphor that we will constantly refer to. It is a reminder of who we truly are.

It's interesting that regardless of the age or the seniority of participants, when we ask them the following question the answers are all uncannily similar.

The question we ask is this: Think of an experience where you felt in the flow. What qualities and emotions were present to you during that time?

We then wait for people to remember an activity or event and how they felt when in the flow.

For some people it is listening to music or playing sport – for others it is being around family – for one man it was taking a bath – for another it was skiing down a slope – being with pets and watching them play.

Regardless of the different experiences, the feelings and qualities that are relayed are all remarkably similar.

Words like these describe the experience: Peace – compassion – connection – timelessness – being in the moment – love – joy – belonging – settledness – contentment.

In the training we then draw a picture of a diamond on a flip chart and write all of these words in green pen in the middle of the diamond.

Soon the diamond is full of beautiful feelings and qualities that seem to resonate with everyone.

Every time we fill in a diamond, I find myself settling

into a space of contentment, just the act of creating the diamond has a wonderful effect.

We then ask the question: "What gets in the way of your Inner Diamond?" A myriad of responses are spoken and they often come thick and fast.

With adults we get things like:

Money – health – career – expectations of others – judgement – self-belief – guilt

With youngsters we get things like:

Exams - friends - fitting in - not being good enough - homework - insecurity - worry.

We write these responses in red pen around the outside of the diamond.

So, at this stage, if you visualise it, there is an image of a diamond that has a series of beautiful words like 'love, joy and contentment' in green in the middle of it and then in red pen, around the outside we have a series of words - like worry, fear, anxiety, money, job, boss, staff, health, the future.

The Inner Diamond, as a metaphor, beautifully sums up what it is to be human.

Your Unbreakable Diamond Core

The core of the diamond is unbreakable.

The qualities of love, joy, resilience and peace are the true essence of who you are – they are at the centre of your very being. These qualities are undamaged and unchanged – they are ever-present.

However, as individuals we experience what it is to be human; the human experience is represented by the red words on the outside of the diamond.

As you place your attention away from your diamond and on to your thinking and worries, you find yourself seemingly moving away from your rock-solid ground.

Instead of feeling peace-of-mind you become lost in the frenzy of fears, insecurity and worry. The red words are like the blustery autumnal storms; they blow in fiercely and at times seem to swamp you.

I used to believe that my True Self was represented by this turbulent, overactive way of being human. However, nothing could be further from the truth.

The red words represent the temporary, Red Thinking (remember the coffee cup) that can sometimes cloud over you.

When you find yourself engaged in an activity that absorbs you fully (like sport, your family, nature or music) you will find that the temporary maelstrom of thinking subsides; this enables the natural well of resilience and security to rise to the surface.

Your True Nature is not the 'thinking storms' that rush over you; your True Nature is the settled space of calm within.

Your True Nature is the witnessing presence of stillness in each moment.

Your True Nature is resilience, wellbeing, love, joy and eternal peace.

However, because you are having a human experience there are times you find yourself lost in the storms and stories of being human.

Do You Know That You Are Sailing Through Life in an Unsinkable Boat?

We were sharing the diamond with a group of school leaders and the group was leaning back on their chairs looking at the flipchart with the green diamond and words of red written around the outside.

"What do you make of that?" asked my husband, Stu.

One of the teachers looked thoughtfully. "I always thought that children could be broken, that they needed fixing. But now I see this diamond I realise that they are unbreakable; you can't break a diamond."

I loved what she said.

She was starting to see something that is rarely explored in everyday conversations. She was starting to see that underneath everything, regardless of how they behaved, underneath it all, the children were psychologically OK.

When children start to see that they are rock-solid at their core, then they start to listen and to trust the wiser, intuitive part of themselves.

When you start to trust that intuitive part of yourself then life is no longer as frightening as it first seemed to be.

One of the symptoms of becoming more curious about your deeper intuitive nature is that you effortlessly feel more settled.

You will be less likely to become lost in the wild, frightening storms of your mind. The insecure and agitated thinking that at one time was to be feared, is now seen as a temporary storm passing through. There is nothing you need to do to fix it.

One of the headteachers I worked with described it like this. He said it was like setting sail in an unsinkable boat. I loved the way he described it. If you set sail in an unsinkable boat, then you would know a couple of things.

Firstly, you would know that you were going to experience rough seas, storms, quiet seas, rain, raging currents and jagged rocks. It's likely there would be times you would be tired, uncomfortable and frightened. However, the second thing you would know is that regardless of the weather or sea conditions your boat was unsinkable. You might feel the fear, but ultimately you would know that you were safe.

Your psychological system is like the boat. You are ultimately unsinkable … Whatever life throws at you, you will be able to take the next step.

Just Take the Next Step and Resilience Will Always Appear

When you 'see' that you are unbreakable, resourceful and resilient you still experience the hurdles and challenges of life.

Life does its things.

You still have to pay the bills, take the kids to school, clean the house and mend the car.

You still experience health issues for yourself or loved ones, and you will still find yourself having moments of insecurity and low self-esteem.

As you experience life in its full glory (with its fears, anxieties and worries) you also notice a natural strength arises. You begin to trust that resilience will show up in whatever way you need it in the moment.

It's like there is a special shaped piece of resilience that is perfect for the situation you find yourself in.

Resilience usually appears in your life in the most ordinary and everyday of ways; it just shows up when you need it and without fanfare.

Let me give you some examples from my long-distance bike-ride across the UK. Resilience showed up in so many different guises every minute of the day.

When I was struggling slowly up the hills on my pushbike, I found myself locking into a rhythmical beat in my head. As I pushed the pedals slowly around, I counted to four and with each count, 'One – Two – Three – Four' I pushed my foot down, it was comforting. The idea to count in a rhythmical way was resilience showing up.

Then on another occasion I was feeling low.

It was pouring with rain and we were wet through and still had several miles to cycle. I could feel the squelch of soggy toes; it was cold and the cars that passed us were spraying us with water.

We were passing through Lancashire and the sign welcoming us said, 'Lancashire a Place Where People Matter.' However, the sign had been vandalised and it actually read: 'Lancashire, a Place Where People Natter.'

In that moment I roared with laughter, in fact I cried with laughter (the tears mingled with the rain).

For some unknown reason this was hilarious to me.

Every time I found myself drifting into moroseness at my situation, the sign would appear in my mind and I would once again laugh loudly.

Resilience had shown up again; it had shown up as laughter and it had given me the perfect tonic for the situation I was in.

I didn't have 'to do' resilience; resilience was naturally occurring in the situation.

Resilience was also present when I visited my husband in Intensive Care.

My husband was on a life-support machine after major surgery. I remember turning up and seeing his body being kept alive by bleeping machines and wires. I feared touching him for pulling out a tube or tangling myself in a wire. Yet in that moment I was present and grounded and I touched his hand and spoke to him. I could do nothing to make him better, but I was able to turn up and be present; that was resilience in action.

When my dad fractured his neck, resilience once again appeared.

We got him to hospital and waited for nearly 10 hours to have him seen. My mum and I had to improvise when it came to toileting him because the staff were so busy. He couldn't move because of his fractured neck, and all the time we had to quietly reassure him (he has dementia) about where he was.

If someone had told me that was going to happen, I would have dreaded my ability to deal with it; however, in each moment resilience appeared and showed me what to do next.

Resilience is always there when you need it.

Resilience is all about taking the next step.

It will always be there in the moment; doing its best to keep you safe and helping you to move forward.

When you absolutely know in your bones that you are made from resilience and that resilience will show you the way in any moment, then you no longer tiptoe through life fearful of what might happen. Instead, you walk through life with a sense of knowing that all will be OK.

There's Nothing to Fix and Nothing to Change

Understanding resilience is at the heart of everything you engage with as Wellbeing Listeners. The Inner Diamond is a good reminder, it's the place to put your attention, both for yourself and others.

But be warned.

You are probably more used to trying to 'fix' and find solutions. You will be more used to listening out to the stuff of thinking, the Red Thinking of worries and fears and insecurities. You have become so used to trying to fix these both in yourself and others, that it will take a bit of time to get out of the habit.

The good news is that as you begin to really see the power of the Inner Diamond in yourself, then you can't help but see it in abundance in others.

When you see the deeper, intuitive intelligence in yourself, then when you listen to others, you'll find yourself connecting to the intelligence within them. As you connect with it you are blowing on their flames of resilience and they start to feel it too.

Summary

- You never experience exactly the same thing as someone else. We all live in our own individual reality.

- We're taught to chase wellbeing and to build resilience. This is a waste of time. Resilience and wellbeing are built-in.

- The Inner Diamond is a metaphor that describes your built-in resilience and wellbeing. Your natural settled state can be described with words like connection, compassion, contentment and gratitude. These words describe your True Nature.

- Your insecure thoughts get in the way of you experiencing the calm space of the diamond. These insecure thoughts distract your attention away from who you truly are (peace, love and calm).

- When you start to trust the Inner Diamond, you experience more ease in your life. You aren't side-tracked so much by your insecure thoughts and fears.

• Resilience is always present in your life. It will show up in whatever shape is needed at the moment. Resilience will always show you the next step, whatever circumstances you find yourself in.

• As a Wellbeing Listener as soon as you start to trust your own built-in wellbeing and resilience, you will automatically see it in the people you are with.

FAQs
The coffee-cup story is very low-key.
What about serious situations like domestic abuse?

We use the analogy of the coffee cup to illustrate how your moods will impact your experience of the world. It is an everyday example that enables people to identify with the shifting and changing nature of moods. I bet you too have an example of the 'coffee cup' in your life.

The same psychological system is at work with everyone, regardless of your situation and what is going on in your world. Everyone else, along with us, will have a psychological experience of the world through their thinking. This means that even if you are in a challenging situation, you will experience your world through your thinking. There are no exceptions. We are always experiencing the world through thought. The problems occur when you don't understand the nature and difference of Red and Green Thinking. That's when you might find yourself prolonging your moments of distress.

Red Thinking is a warning sign. It isn't telling you about your circumstances. Your feelings are letting you know about your thinking at the moment. When you are agitated you will experience an agitated world.

Red Thinking is alerting you to look within; to seek out

the settled space of wisdom and clarity within. Your agitated feelings are letting you know not to trust your thinking in the moment; they are alerting you to the fact that your attention has strayed from your Inner Diamond.

What I've noticed over the years is that if you don't understand the nature of agitated, unsettled thinking then you might become stuck in thought-storms and habitual thoughts.

However, when you start to distinguish the difference between the urgent, agitation of Red Thinking and the calmer, wiser knowing of awareness, then you naturally start to trust your intuitive wisdom.

In other words, you listen to your Inner Diamond.

From this space you make healthy decisions about life. When you are in Green Thinking it means you have less on your mind, there is less agitation of thought and as a result the quieter, nourishing voice of awareness is more likely to be heard.

For example, I listened to someone who was experiencing domestic abuse for many years. She wasn't in any physical danger, but she endured abuse on a daily basis. One day, in a moment of clarity, she realised things weren't healthy and she sought advice from a help-group. From this space of Green Thinking she realised that she needed to communicate some boundaries to her partner, which she did, and they are now seeking to find a way of navigating life differently. When she was lost in Red Thinking, she found herself stuck; when she trusted her intuitive wisdom, she made some healthy choices about living life differently.

Your role as a Wellbeing Listener is to tune in to that resilience and wisdom in yourself and then from that space you tune in to the resilience of the other person. When you get in touch with your Inner Diamond you are able to shine a light on the Inner Diamond in the other. That's when they start to trust that the answers lie within.

In Action: Listening With Compassion Rather Than Ego

Here's Russell, a Deputy Headteacher, describing how Wellbeing Listening turned up for him in the workplace. He remembers a staff meeting when an initiative he was planning to implement at school was not being warmly received by everyone.

"It didn't take me long to notice that on one particular table there was a teacher who was clearly quite worked-up. Her body language was negative, and her tone was one of frenetic concern. I decided to head over to see if I could help.

The first thing I noticed was how the colleagues sitting around her were being absorbed into her story about how difficult the initiative would be to implement. Before I knew about Inside-Out, my more combative, persuasive 'mode' would kick-in and I'd be up for the battle. But with my understanding of Inside-Out, I simply observed that some of my colleagues were in insecure thinking and needed to be heard.

So, I asked them to tell me what they were thinking. I acknowledged their worries. Instead of responding from a defensive place (my ego) I listened with compassion.

When I sensed that my colleagues felt heard, I was then able to calmly talk through some practical tips that I knew would work for them. I ended up feeling really supported by my colleagues because my 'groundedness' had them settle down and see the situation clearly.

I actually only became conscious of how I responded to this situation when my Assistant Head pointed it out to me after the meeting. She said, 'I couldn't believe how calm you were when they got all worked up! I would have been really defensive and gone about persuading them they were wrong.'

This was a really nice example of how Inside-Out had shifted the way I went about introducing changes in my school. In my job I have come to accept that people will often have anxious thinking. I don't respond from my ego, but instead listen with compassion.

When people feel heard, they almost always feel more ready to listen deeply and respond from a place of clarity. Very often, there's no issue to deal with at all. The story is just... a story."

Your Turn

Can you remember a time when you felt up against life? How did you get through that time? Can you remember the ideas that occurred to you? Can you spot your resilience in the tiny and seemingly inconsequential actions?

P.S.

We don't all carry around individual diamonds. I am pointing to something universal that connects us all. The Inner Diamond describes the energy behind life itself. We are like refractions of light that dance in the diamond of life. We are created of and made from the life-force that runs through everyone and everything.

Chapter 4

Listening at the Level of Soul

"All that we seek in this world that is truly lasting – true
happiness, joy, peace, light, space – are inside of us."

Mooji *

Listening to Your Inner Self: Your Hidden Diamond

As I sit down to write this chapter it is a cold, wet winter's day. The log burner is alight and I am sitting on the sofa watching the foggy, wet weather hurl itself against the window.

It is so lovely to move my eye from the wild weather outside to the glow of the log burner's flame. A wave of gratitude washes over me. I feel so snug and warm. My eyes keep shifting to the weather and then back to the roaring fire.

Each time I look outside and then back to the fire I am reminded that this is a special moment.

It is in this lovely warm room, beside the fire, that I prepare to write.

First, I read some of the previous chapters and start to settle myself and my focus inwardly. It is good to look within to find a focused awareness; this is my preferred way to write.

What do I mean by 'focused awareness'?

It's a bit like becoming absorbed in a good book or film. Or it's a bit like shifting through wakefulness to sleep.

---

* From 'Vaster Than Sky Greater Than Space'. Published by Coronet.

There is a space where awareness is removed from the outside world and gently focusses inwards.

It's a space where the outside world is no longer compelling.

As I sink into this reflective space my husband suddenly asks me a question. As he does so I am jolted back into the world. His words have flung a pebble into the still pond of my mind. I answer him, and when the interaction has finished the ripples of my mind settle once again, and I return to the gentle space of concentration to write.

Can you relate to this?

Can you bring to mind a time when you were absorbed in concentration; a time when the outside world ceased to have a hold on you? Can you also recall when this space of calm was suddenly interrupted?

It is like being awoken just as you drift to sleep.

You are forced back into the world of engaging your brain and mind.

A part of you feels a pang of loss. You realise that the beautiful space you were inhabiting has been snatched away. You long to return, but you can't do that by becoming busy with your thinking; instead, you allow yourself to become calm.

When the ripples on the pond lose their energy, then you are able to return to that settled space of being.

When we talk about listening to the Inner Diamond we are talking about this kind of listening.

It is not a busy-minded active thing you 'do'.

It is a settled space of awareness that you return to.

There is a distinction between listening to the Inner Diamond and listening to your thoughts; it *feels different*. There is a contrast between the settled space of awareness and the alert, active mind.

For me I can discern the difference through my feelings.

When I listen to my thoughts, I often feel an agitation and a need to 'do' something or 'think' something out. I might feel energetic and I find myself zapping around.

Sometimes my active thinking is exhausting, as thoughts rush into my head demanding attention.

It feels different when I listen to my Inner Diamond. My Diamond feels more like a 'knowing' rather than an agitated feeling.

When you start listening to yourself and to your Inner Diamond you'll notice how nourishing it feels. Many people on the Wellbeing Listener Programme are exhausted, they feel beholden to others. There is often a sense of responsibility; to prioritise the wellbeing of others over their own.

At the end of the Wellbeing Listener Training people are often surprised. They expected to learn how to listen to others and yet what they're seeing is that listening starts much closer to home.

The first place to look for the Inner Diamond is in yourself. As you start to notice your Inner Diamond you will discover that you feel energised and nurtured.

A beautiful thing happens when you listen to your Inner Diamond. As you start to trust and see your wholeness, then your listening for others naturally shifts and you see the wholeness in others.

As you intuitively 'feel' your Inner Diamond then it seems to act like a magnet. People are drawn to you. You are radiating a sense of contentment, calm and connection. Those in distress often seek out someone who is standing on solid ground.

One of our Wellbeing Listeners described it like this:

"My Inner Diamond is a big ball of positive energy. It is the thing that connects me to everyone else. It's a little like the molten fire that we have at the core of the earth. The hard mantle, the surface layer is what people can see and touch and what we often label. The core is something we know is there but it's covered up and as a result we often forget about it or don't realise its importance until it breaks through! It's that breaking through that people then take notice of and on some deep, unspoken level people can intuitively feel that my Inner Diamond has been rediscovered (and polished!) and it seems to draw them towards it.

I haven't made any changes to my outer layer so why would they reach out now? It must be because they have noticed a shift in my inner energy and therefore my responses to situations."

As you listen in for your Inner Diamond you will realise your connection to this deeper energy of resourcefulness, wisdom and resilience.

Acting from a Place of Spaciousness

When I listen to that settled, spaciousness of awareness (the Inner Diamond) then I am 'being.'

This sense of 'being' feels good; there is no need to get busy 'doing' something.

Actions might occur, but these actions seem natural and unfolding, they are not forced or agitated.

From this space of being I write, from this space of being I listen, from this space of being I hang out with my loved ones.

I don't feel an urgency to be understood or acknowledged.

From this space of being I feel a sense of connection and ease.

It might sound like you're either in a 'settled' space or

in an 'agitated' space. That's not my experience. Regardless of the moods, thoughts and feelings I'm always able to look inward for that space of settled peace.

As soon as I 'notice' that I've become lost in my thinking and mood then an insight sparks up.

This spark of insight takes the form of 'noticing'; I notice my mood.

This noticing is my Inner Compass nudging me back. My Inner Compass is reminding me that I'm looking for peace-of-mind in the wrong direction.

The world might be chaotic and my moods might be erratic. But in the same way that my eyes glance away from the raging weather outside the window to the warmth of the fire inside, so my inner eye shifts away from the raging moods and places its attention on the spacious observer.

When you experience life from the perspective of the spacious observer you feel a sense of nourishment, regardless of your feelings.

I remember a Wellbeing Listener once asking me a question. She was confused. Her aunt was very ill and in hospital. She was feeling upset, but this sense of sadness felt 'right' and she couldn't understand why.

"I feel upset, but I feel OK. Surely if I'm feeling unhappy I'm in Red Thinking? This feeling of upset feels healthy. Why does it feel healthy to feel upset?"

This Wellbeing Listener was sharing something powerful. You might feel sad, distressed or overwhelmed but if you are experiencing these feelings from the perspective of your settled awareness, then these emotions aren't debilitating. In fact, these feelings often have a sense of healthiness to them.

Wellbeing Listening is not about feeling happy all the time. Wellbeing Listening is about experiencing the whole range of emotions and knowing these feelings aren't who you truly are. As you observe your emotions from a settled space of awareness you experience a sense of nourishment and wholeness.

The Rotten Tree and the Trap of Believing Everything You Think

One day whilst out walking I noticed my neighbour had taken down a tree. The tree had rotted and was potentially dangerous, so he had brought in a tree surgeon to remove it.

There was just a tree stump left when I walked past. I asked him how the tree-felling had gone.

"Yesterday was terribly stressful," my neighbour told me. He then went on to explain how worried he'd been. He was worried that the tree surgeon was going to fall out of the tree; he was worried that the tree surgeon might cut his leg with the chainsaw; he was worried that an ambulance would take so long to attend that he might bleed to death and he was worried that they would be culpable for his death.

I could see from the way he was talking that he was feeling distressed and anxious.

"Did the tree surgeon hurt himself?" I asked curiously. "No, but I worried all day about him, it could have been terrible," he responded.

My neighbour shows how easy it is to fall into the trap of believing your thinking.

He found it hard to discern the difference between reality and imagination. During the previous day he had had a full-blown experience of:

- A tree surgeon who had fallen from the tree.
- A tree surgeon who had cut his leg and bled to death.
- An ambulance that couldn't make it to the house in time.

- A court case where he'd been accused of causing the death of the tree surgeon.

No wonder he was stressed! What actually happened is this: *The tree surgeon did a good job of felling the tree.*

My neighbour was listening to the fearful stories in his head. He was scaring himself.

If my neighbour had understood that he was in Red Thinking he would have mistrusted what his feelings and thoughts were telling him. If he'd realised that his agitated feelings were a reminder that he was looking in the wrong direction for peace-of-mind, then he would have looked inwards and listened to the settled space within.

The secret to listening is to know what to listen out for and what to ignore. When we listen out for love, then we hear love. When we listen out for resilience, then we hear resilience. When we listen out for fear then we hear fear.

Whatever we listen out for becomes amplified.

As a Wellbeing Listener you are tuning to your Inner Diamond. As you tune in and notice the Inner Diamond (both in yourself and others) the louder the Inner Diamond seems to get.

It reminds me of mushrooming with my brother.

He's a keen 'mushroomer' and in the autumn he loves picking chanterelles. These orange fungi grow amongst the leaf litter in woods. To the untrained eye they are hard to spot amongst the golden carpet of fallen leaves.

Whilst walking in the forest he often points to what looks like a pile of leaves. The chanterelles are so well camouflaged that at first, despite straining my eyes, I can't see them.

As the walk progresses, things begin to change and I start to notice the mushrooms more quickly. Then, at last, I spot a chanterelle before he does; I feel elation. It has taken some time, but when my eye was trained, I was able to spot them.

This chanterelle experience reminds me of Wellbeing Listening. In the same way that I was able to start noticing the chanterelles once my eyes were accustomed, so you will be able to spot resilience, resourcefulness and wellbeing when your listening is tuned to your Inner Diamond.

If you tune in to the qualities of the Inner Diamond then peace-of-mind, love and kindness seem louder; if you tune in to fear and insecurity then those feelings seem to escalate.

Like the chanterelles, love, resilience, compassion and wellbeing are already present, but initially can be hard to see.

Failing to Listen Means Failing to Connect

Have you ever been to a social event where someone asks you what you do and then glazes over as you answer? When it happens to me I dry up completely, I find it nearly impossible to speak.

We've all had experiences of not being listened to.

My husband and I used to run a listening exercise when we were Coaching Skills trainers.

We'd ask the group to pair off and for one person to listen to the other. Then part way through this exercise the 'listener' would be instructed to look disinterested, bored or distracted.

As soon as the listener stopped listening then the impact on the speaker was extraordinary. The speaker went from talking with passion and ease to stuttering and faltering.

It was incredible to witness the difference between someone who felt listened to and someone who was not being listened to.

The participants often declared that this would never happen in real life, that they would never stop listening to someone.

The truth is we've all done it; I know that I am guilty of this too.

Sometimes, when I am running late and a friend calls me wanting to chat, I don't listen properly because I'm feeling rushed.

There are times when a friend is in full flow and she says something that reminds me of a similar incident, then I might hijack the conversation and tell her about my thing.

On one occasion I was in front of a group talking about the importance of listening. One of the participants was sharing a story when I heard a beeping noise. My mind started to fill up with the concerns that my computer battery was about to die. After 30 seconds I realised that I hadn't heard a word of what had been said. It was unintentional, but the irony doesn't escape me; here I was teaching people to listen whilst simultaneously falling into the trap of not listening.

Often when you fail to listen it's because you're distracted with the noise in your head.

Your internal voice is piping up commentating on what is being said; it may be judging, or coming up with fixes and solutions. Often your internal voice is comparing what's being said with your own bank of memories.

It's hard to listen when you've got so much noise going on in your mind.

Noticing the Noise in Your Head

We all do it. If you're anything like me then much of your life is spent lost in agitated thinking. I bet you have a running commentary of what you are feeling or about what you think you should say or do.

Often my commentary informs me to feel anxious about not being liked. Or I become annoyed at how others behave, or I imagine fearful scenarios of the future or regurgitate unsettling memories from the past.

Does this happen to you? I bet that most of the time you don't even notice the noise in your head; you become used to it. It took a while for me to realise that I didn't listen as well as I might because of my head-noise.

A big misconception about listening is to believe that it is your responsibility to make others feel better.

Most of the self-help books tell you that feelings like overwhelm, insecurity and low self-esteem are wrong.

Many self-help practitioners urge you to think positively, or to change your mood and state-of-mind. They offer tips, tools and strategies to do this.

The message you are told time and again in our culture is that it is wrong to feel one way and that you should instead feel something else.

When you listen to others, it can be easy to transfer these self-help messages onto them. You think other people shouldn't feel the way they feel and it's down to you to help make them feel better and fix them.

There is something else available to you regardless of your loud thinking. We call this 'something else' your Inner Compass.

Your Inner Compass is Always Guiding You

Have you noticed that regardless of the mental noise there is always a part of you that longs for inner calm?

Your Inner Compass is always at work, it's reminding you to focus your attention away from the exhaustion of turmoiled thinking and to instead locate the Inner Diamond within.

Your Inner Compass is pointing you back towards peace-of-mind.

When someone comes to you in agitated thinking, they too want to reconnect to their peace-of-mind.

Their Inner Compass is nudging them towards a conversation where they can be heard.

They don't need to try to become a better person, all they need is to allow the ripples of their mind to settle and to touch base with the ever-present unchanging part of themselves.

Many people I listen to are frightened because they misunderstand how life works.

These people don't realise that their thinking can create a web of fear and anxiety, and this web of fear bears no relation to what is actually happening in the real world.

Many people I listen to are struggling to release themselves from the fearful stories they create, but like the fly that is caught in the spider's web, their struggling just entangles them more.

When someone is heard, their mind settles.

Listening to someone is an act of love.

Your Role as a Wellbeing Listener

As a Wellbeing Listener you tune in to the resilience and wellbeing in the other person. It makes no sense to become lost in the story or to whip it up further.

With my neighbour and his story about the tree surgeon, I UNDERSTOOD what was going on.

He was lost in a frightening world of thought and it seemed true.

- He believed that the tree felling had caused his distress.
- He didn't know that the extra layers of thinking he added were making him even more stressed.
- He thought he needed to 'fix' his thinking with more thinking.
- He had lost sight of his settled, calm True Nature.

My role as a Wellbeing Listener was to:

- Listen without adding more fuel to his story.
- Recognise that he had felt stressed, but to not lose myself in his stress.
- Keep my eyes peeled for his grounded resilience and resourcefulness.

In this instance it made sense for me to:

- Acknowledge that he'd been wise to remove the dangerous tree.
- Admire the work of the tree surgeon.

If he had been on a Wellbeing Listener course, then I would have gone further.

If someone is on a Wellbeing Listener course, then you have permission to gently challenge; you don't have that permission in everyday conversations.

On a Wellbeing Listener course, I might have explored how his thoughts had felt frightening and stressful. I might have become curious at the stark difference between the stories that frightened him and what had actually happened.

On a Wellbeing Listener Training I would have been helping him see his Red Thinking. I would also be inviting him to explore the part of him that was noticing and witnessing the Red Thinking.

On a Wellbeing Listener training I would be gently nudging him to be curious about seeing something about his True Nature.

The Beauty of Being Heard

When you feel truly heard there is a deep ease and relief.

My dad is elderly, frail and has dementia and there are times I feel very sad that the dad I once knew is no longer there.

When I talk to people and express my sadness there are few who actually listen and are present.

Everyone wants to help and to be kind, but they don't realise I just want to be heard.

I've noticed that people often feel uncomfortable when I'm in 'unsettled thinking'. They take this as a signal to cheer me up or to find a solution.

When I express sadness about Dad, people often switch the story to their parents, or they offer suggestions on respite care or they recommend carers, or they suggest I read a dementia book.

I remember talking to someone once and she just listened. She was deeply present and at the end of it she said, "Liz it sounds tough. And I can see that you deeply care for your parents. You really love them don't you?"

When she said this, I cried.

I was deeply touched.

Her capacity to sit and listen to me had enabled me to feel that space of connection and love within. She realised that I wasn't looking for answers or solutions, I just wanted to be heard.

I wanted to be heard at the level of soul.

It really does something when you listen in this way.

Learning to Listen is Learning to Connect: The Do's and Don'ts

If you can listen to someone without becoming caught up in their agitated thoughts, then you are on the way to being a Wellbeing Listener.

The role of a Wellbeing Listener is to point in the right direction.

A Wellbeing Listener doesn't need to teach or instruct.

A Wellbeing Listener doesn't need to talk about Red and Green Thinking, Inner Diamonds or True Nature.

All you need to do as a Wellbeing Listener is listen.

But what exactly is listening?

Let's see what listening is not.

Listening is not about getting lost in someone's story.

Listening is not about trying to fix or change the other person's mind.

Listening is not about memorising what is being said or offering ideas and solutions.

Listening is not about telling the person about something similar in your life.

What is listening?

Listening is about sensing the grounded space of peace within you and feeling and connecting to that grounded space of peace in the other person.

As you listen in to your Inner Diamond, you'll connect with the Inner Diamond of the person you're with.

My Inner Diamond is your Inner Diamond. It is made of the same stuff. I know your Inner Diamond, because I know mine.

Of course, there aren't actually two Diamonds, there is just one.

This one *Diamond* is the life-force energy and awareness behind life itself.

When I listen from the space of my Inner Diamond, then I am listening deeply.

It means that I am listening from behind my mask to behind your mask.

Listening is about noticing the peace within your own mind and listening out for the wisdom that arises in others.

That wisdom will nudge you to say something, or to be quiet.

That wisdom will remind you to not get lost in stories or try to fix the person you're with.

As you listen and feel your own wisdom and wellbeing, then you will naturally tune into the wisdom and wellbeing of the other person.

Listening is what naturally happens when the flurry of thoughts, the noise of beliefs and the buzz of 'shoulds and should nots' settle down.

Listening and presence is all that's left when our thinking recedes.

This is the kind of listening we're encouraging Wellbeing Listeners to aspire to.

This is the kind of listening that the world is thirsty for.

This is the kind of listening that enables others to feel heard.

This kind of listening is love in action.

Summary

- You can experience your Inner Diamond through a focussed awareness.

- You can feel the difference between listening to your Inner Diamond and listening to your agitated thinking.

- If you become lost in agitated thinking you will believe the world is frightening and you'll find life mentally exhausting.

- Your agitated feelings look like they're telling you about an agitated world – they aren't. Your agitated feelings are letting you know you are in agitated thinking.

- These agitated feelings are not telling you what to 'fix' in your world. Your agitated thinking is letting you know that you are looking for clarity and peace-of-mind in the wrong direction. The right direction is to reconnect with your Inner Diamond.

- A Wellbeing Listener keeps an eye open for the constant, ever-present stillness within. You will see that regardless of your thoughts, feelings and moods, the space of stillness is always there.

- When you listen to your Inner Diamond you touch base with your wellbeing and resilience and when you listen out for the Inner Diamond in others, they touch base with their own inner resilience and wellbeing.

- Compassion and empathy naturally arise when you realise that someone is lost in Red Thinking. You feel compassion because you know that you too get lost in insecure thinking. You feel empathy because you know it is uncomfortable and frightening to be lost in Red Thinking.

- Wellbeing listening is not about fixing or giving advice. Wellbeing Listening is about being present with another person. Being present is the greatest of gifts you can give to someone.

FAQs

Why do I still get wound up with people I love if I'm a Wellbeing Listener?

Variations on this question are very common. People feel that when they know about Wellbeing Listening, then they should be immune to feeling angry or frustrated. If they feel annoyed with others, then they blame themselves for being a bad Wellbeing Listener.

However, Wellbeing Listening is not a strategy to be a good person, it is not a technique for self-development. Wellbeing Listening is a description of what it is to be human. As you better understand the human dynamic, you'll find yourself noticing the times you listen well and the times when your listening is poor.

You are human and there will be times when you are lost in Red Thinking. This Red Thinking might be insecurity, worry, anxiety or frustration etc, and your outside world will reflect whatever you're feeling. If you attempt to listen to others when you're in Red Thinking, then your ability to listen will be impaired.

When I am in Red Thinking, I know I'm not in a good place to listen. Sometimes, just this act of noticing is all that is needed to help my mind to settle. On other occasions I might take myself off for a walk, or take a few deep breaths, or go and lie down; I'll do whatever feels right.

There are also occasions when I'm in Red Thinking and I respond from that place. I am snappy and annoyed, or I listen badly to others. If I fall into the trap of bad listening (and I'm human so I do) then whilst I might regret my actions later, I don't beat myself up. I know my Red Thinking doesn't tell me anything about my True Nature (of peace, love and compassion).

As a Wellbeing Listener you'll start to notice more quickly when you're in Red Thinking.

As a Wellbeing Listener, as your thinking settles, you'll realise what has been going on. From this space of settled Green Thinking you'll do what needs to be done. If you've listened badly to someone you might need to apologise or take time to listen again. Rather than beat yourself up you'll also start to notice a feeling of understanding towards yourself.

It's very likely, if you're human, that you will continue to:

a) Get flustered/annoyed and angry with others.

b) When you get flustered/annoyed and angry you will experience a world that mirrors your thoughts and feelings.

However…

As a Wellbeing Listener, you won't pile on additional guilt, frustration or annoyance. You'll pause and allow the feelings to settle and re-engage when it feels right to do so.

As a Wellbeing Listener you will also notice that:

a) You'll catch on to your feelings more quickly.

b) You'll realise that your feelings are letting you know what colour glasses you're wearing at any one time.

c) You are not your feelings (there is a deeper awareness within).

d) As soon as you 'notice' your feelings you are on the way to settled thinking.

We're all human, we feel it all. There are no feelings we need to be frightened of. Feelings and thoughts come and go, we are not our feelings and thoughts, we are that which is the awareness and the observer of them all.

In Action: The Teacher That Stopped Finding Solutions

Angie is a teacher working with teenagers. At first she couldn't understand why so many troubled students were seeking her out. She didn't see that she was 'doing' anything other than listening.

Soon students were being sent to her from the student referral unit. The student referral unit is the place that students go when they feel troubled or are displaying challenging behaviour. The unit sent students to Angie because she was making a real difference to those she was seeing.

Angie began to realise that the biggest difference she was making was not what she was saying. She didn't talk about Red or Green Thinking or Diamonds. As she says, it wasn't what she was doing, the real difference was *the place she was listening from.*

She goes on to say:

"It's about me and how I'm different with the students and teachers. At some level they sense there is something very different in me. The place I was coming from before was fixing and offering solutions, but that's never been needed."

When Angie is with the students she is listening from a settled space and she knows deeply in her heart that these students might be in troubled Red Thinking, but there is nothing that is ultimately wrong with them.

One student, who was very anxious and worried because of her parent's break-up, came to talk to Angie. At the end of this conversation, the girl went from being anxious to realising that her parents' relationship with each other was not for her to fix. She left the conversation feeling settled and resourced.

Angie said that she just listens.

"I'm just really still with them and I don't engage in the stories or pour any fuel on the stories, I just listen. I'm really listening to them."

What she then noticed is that the students move away from anxiety and their mind quietens. From a quiet mind they then come to their own conclusions.

Your Turn

Can you notice the difference between the agitated thoughts and thoughts arising from clarity? The agitated thoughts will be full of judgement, guilt or insecurity. They will overwhelm you. When your Red Thinking 'instructs' you to do something, it's wise to pause. On the other hand, your thoughts arising from clarity are settled, knowing and clear. The behaviour that follows from Green Thinking can be trusted. Can you notice the difference for yourself?

P.S.

You can't escape from or lose that settled sense of awareness. It is always with you, regardless of your mood or thinking. See if you can notice the space within you that is untouched by your mood. This isn't about feeling better or happier, this is about noticing an ever-present energy within.

Chapter 5

When Feeling Good
Becomes Natural

"For the most part, we are suffering collectively from intellectual over-stimulation and soul under-nourishment. Facts and figures might provide useful information, but when the deeper need is for transformation, only soul-food can help with that."
Ian Watson *

The Confusion of Natural v Normal

I was in a classroom sharing a message about wellbeing and resilience.

I glanced at the teacher and felt concerned.

The students were in a full flowing conversation about stress, anxiety and worry. They'd been scribbling on flip chart paper and swapping stories about the pressure of exams and home learning. They'd been discussing bullying, fall-outs with friends and they'd been expressing fear that if they don't do well in exams, they might be messing up their whole lives.

Every time I tried to steer the discussion towards resilience, the students steered it back to stress.

The weight and insecurity of their conversation stunned me.

As I looked at the teacher I wondered if she'd intervene; was she as surprised as me?

---

* From Ian Watson's blog published at theinsightspace.com

Here were a group of aspirational, funny, kind, intelligent teenagers sharing openly about a world that seemed burdensome and heavy.

The teacher was dedicated to her students. Surely, she would step in and help point them back to their resilience again.

A fifteen-year-old girl, who had just shared how she had felt mentally paralysed with the amount of study required suddenly piped up. "I wish I were young again," she said wistfully. "I wish I were back at primary school, playing in the playground, back then I enjoyed life."

The girl's observation struck me to the core. How could someone so young, bright and caring find life so hard?

I tried to catch the teacher's eye, but rather than expressing shock she nodded in agreement. She didn't dispute their world of over-work, lack of sleep and fear. I realised with a jolt that the teacher was swimming in the same world as the students. They were all swimming in a world of stress and none of them could see how unhealthy this was.

They believed that this was how life was supposed to be.

This group had normalised stress and they believed stress was their natural default setting.

No wonder these students were mentally drained. They'd muddled up the definitions of 'natural' and 'normal'. The stress they felt had been normalised, but it was not natural. They had been living their lives with a big misunderstanding.

Can Feeling Good Become the Norm?

Six months later there was a huge difference with the very same students who were earlier gripped with stress. These same students stood on a conference stage and shared the impact of living without the fear of stress.

One seventeen-year-old lad described how he had gone from being; "In a constant state of stress and panic," to "feeling free." He went on to say that he could now see that the 'shackles' holding him down were "merely an illusion." The illusion he was referring to was thought.

A fifteen-year-old described that prior to the Wellbeing Group she'd been impacted by a series of panic attacks. These attacks had been frightening, she'd been to a counsellor. Now, after being in the group she noticed that the panic attacks had gone. She hadn't tried to make them go; they had gone of their own accord.

One after another these students (the same ones who'd been swimming in that sea of stress just a few months earlier), shared their journey from worry to a settled mind.

What had happened? What had caused such an incredible turn-around?

One of the sixteen-year-old students described it perfectly. She said of the Wellbeing Group, "This group has taught me that our natural state is happiness, we're born to be happy. It is only our thoughts that make us feel what we're feeling."

What she said is worth repeating. It is so incredibly wise, she said:

"This group has taught me that our natural state is happiness, we're born to be happy. It is only our thoughts that make us feel what we're feeling."

These students had made a shift from understanding what was 'normal' and what was 'natural'.

Six months earlier, stress and worry seemed to be a normal part of life. Now, after touching base with their Inner Diamond, they recognised something else. This 'something else' was a recognition of what was natural. They realised that their natural state was happiness, they were 'born to be happy'.

Time and again we see that when you fall back into what is natural, then you are able to align yourself with how life actually works. The first step of this journey is to notice that the constant swirl of stress, worry and anxiety isn't natural.

The Power of Your Natural IQ

If you want to better understand this deeper, natural, intuitive intelligence then take a look at Nature. She is a great teacher.

For a couple of years, a pair of swallows nested in our garage. I watched in awe when the pair returned from their 3,000-mile journey from Africa, to find their old nest.

Over the weeks we witnessed them sit on eggs, feed their young and then take the fledglings out for practice flights in the outside world.

When magpies appeared in the garden, the parent swallows chattered angrily and would bravely fly around, distracting the magpies from the nest.

Bearing witness to this was inspiring. How did they do it? How did they know how to find their old nest, how to raise chicks, how to deal with predators? What was 'the inner knowing' they were following?

This is just a simple illustration of the powerful, foundational, invisible intelligence that is at work.

When I plant a seed and watch the shoots unfurl, I am awestruck at the miracle of what is happening. When I watch a new-born lamb nudge its mother for milk, or see a buzzard catch the thermals and glide effortlessly up, then these daily miracles remind me of the deeper intelligence behind life.

Nature doesn't read books or memorise facts. Nature is an expression of this natural intelligence.

In the heart of our village is a wildflower meadow. At the height of summer, it is a swaying mass of tall grasses with the sharp reds of poppies and the hazy blues of cornflowers peeping through.

Butterflies and bees flit around and if you look closely you can see insects and beetles clinging on to the bowing heads of grasses.

Beside this wildflower meadow the lawn has been clipped short. It is smart, regulated and neat. What a contrast to the flowing, evolving meadow.

When I see the meadow my heart soars.

There is such freedom, life and natural energy that is being expressed through the wide variety of plants. When

Nature is allowed to flourish, she is spectacular in her artistry.

Five years ago, I would have favoured an orderly lush, green lawn. In my world tightly clipped grass was normal. Neat lawns were 'better' than messy grass. Nowadays, my mind has reversed. It is the natural flowing meadows that I see as healthy.

Have You Normalised Stress?

It is the same with your mind. Ask yourself if you have normalised something that isn't healthy. If you're anything like me you were raised to see that full minds, with active thinking and a speedy intellect, were desirable.

Here are some of the things I've noticed people have normalised.

- A whirring and busy mind.
- Endlessly worrying about the future.
- Dissecting and analysing the past.
- Being forgetful and tired.
- Snapping at people you love.
- Waking up at night with thoughts churning.
- Flitting from task to task.

Normalising a life like this is turning your back on what is natural. You aren't designed to live like this and the repercussions are endless.

A teacher was sent to me because she'd had a panic attack. She said that her panic attack had come from 'nowhere'. However, during our first session it became clear that for months on end she'd been finding it hard to sleep, she'd been working all hours, she was short-tempered with her partner, she was getting forgetful and she was turning her friends away because she was 'too busy at work'.

These were all signs that her body was giving her, warning her that she was in an unhealthy space. However, she had misread the signs. She thought she needed to overcome them. She thought these signs were showing her that she wasn't good at managing a busy job.

As we gently explored the signs her body had displayed she gradually began to see that her panic attack hadn't come 'out of nowhere'. Her panic attack was a very understandable response to a revved-up and tired mind.

You are living in a culture where over-thinking has been normalised.

It is common for people we meet to believe that stress, pressure, worry and agitation are 'just the way life is'. This isn't true.

The Relief of Living from What's Natural

Many people who are spinning a multitude of mental plates, are looking for tools and techniques to be better plate spinners. They don't want to slow their lives down; they want to find ways of being more proficient at living at a high speed.

Part of the role of the Wellbeing Listener is to help people recognise the signs of over-thinking. Part of the role of the Wellbeing Listener is to help people understand the difference between what is natural (their Inner Diamond), and what they have normalised (stress, anxiety and non-stop busyness).

As you help people reconnect to their Inner Diamond, they naturally start to take good care of themselves.

I remember coaching a manager in a factory who couldn't sit still because of the agitation of his thinking. His job was excessively busy, and he was feeling the pressure of having to respond to staff and to keep the factory production lines going.

At first, he was convinced he needed to find smarter ways to work and to be more effective with his time management. His mind was leaping around, flitting from thought to thought, it was exhausting to hear.

As his mind settled (minds settle when you listen for wellbeing), he started to realise that he was leading an unhealthy life.

He realised he needed to seek help from his boss, and he needed to take a holiday from work.

From a space of settled resourcefulness he naturally knew what he needed to do next.

It's so easy to under-estimate the power of listening.

Listening seems to help people reconnect with something healthy and natural; you connect with your Inner Diamond.

When you experience the Inner Diamond, your thinking starts to settle and you naturally make healthy decisions.

One day my husband Stu answered the phone to an overworked, exhausted teacher. A mutual friend was concerned about her mental health and had given her Stu's number. She phoned out of the blue because she was feeling under immense stress and pressure.

For an hour I heard Stu making affirmative noises, he was letting her know that he was listening. He didn't say much other than saying, 'hmm' and 'yes' and 'oh'.

There were times he would say things like, "Wow, what you did then was really resourceful." Or "I can really see your resilience coming through there".

He was deeply listening to her wellbeing and from his settled Inner Diamond space he was able to connect with her, as he did so she settled.

She went from agitated 'normalised' over-thinking, to a settled slower space.

In this settled space she was able to respond to that quiet voice of wisdom within, she could hear what she needed.

That voice of wisdom was her Inner Diamond communicating.

At the end of the call, the teacher realised she needed to take time off. She realised she was on the verge of a mental meltdown and that she needed time to rest and recuperate.

She had discovered her natural space of resilience within and she had had some fresh thinking emerge through insights.

When you listen for the wellbeing in another person then you provide a great environment for insights to emerge. It is insight which leads you on the most direct route back to your natural state of balance and ease.

When Insight and Intellect Work Together as Best Friends

Insights are another aspect of this effortless, natural intelligence. You learn so much through your insights, yet I was never taught about insights until just a few years ago.

Insights are an easeful, deeper form of intelligence.

As a Wellbeing Listener you are creating conditions that are conducive to insights.

Insights are so ordinary and everyday that you often overlook and dismiss them.

When I look into my nearly empty fridge wondering what to make for tea and an idea pops into my head, that idea comes through an insight. When my step-son, a carpenter, suddenly sees an answer to a complicated building project, that answer comes through insight. It is an insight that lets me know when I'm thirsty (so I have a drink), it's an insight that helps me see an answer to a crossword puzzle, it is an insight that nudges me to send a card to a friend in need.

An insight occurs when you see through a cloud of confused thinking.

Here on Dartmoor, the mists can come down and obscure the landscape.

When you walk in the mist you can only see a few metres ahead. When the mist lifts and the sun shines through, the whole landscape becomes clear.

This is like an insight.

Most of us are taught to use our minds and to sharpen our intellects.

Great value is placed on passing exams, learning information and quickly finding answers to problems. Your intellectual mind is a great servant, but your intellectual mind is a poor master. If you only rely on your intellect to

guide you, then it is like living with a hand tied behind your back. You're missing out on balancing the intellect with insights.

The intellect is great at making lists and remembering facts. The intellect is great at writing plans and interpreting data.

However, if you want to live a free, spacious and easy life, then 'the intellect' on its own is not the answer.

When you couple the power of intellect with the power of insights then life runs more freely.

A friend of mine is a solicitor. He is supremely-intellectually sharp and has a vast database of legal knowledge in his head. When he is with a client, he describes the way he engages. He says he settles down and listens. As he listens to the client, he doesn't actively get busy in his head. He keeps focussing on the client and he keeps listening. As he does so the pieces of legal knowledge he needs pop into his mind. His intellect is the servant of insight.

Insights usually appear out of nowhere. An insight often arrives without you trying to find it.

I remember a teacher who was having her lesson observed. Teachers often dislike lesson observations. They worry that they might be judged by those watching the lesson.

On this particular day as the teacher was delivering her lesson, she suddenly had an insight into what the class needed. The insight was to play the children a piece of classical music so they could describe what they felt as they heard it. The idea to play the music wasn't on her lesson plan. She could feel her intellect pulling her back to her lesson plan, her intellect didn't want her to play the music. But she knew to trust her insight; she knew what the class needed at that moment.

After the lesson she wondered if she would be judged harshly by those observing her. She hadn't kept to the plan. To her surprise the opposite was the case. Her lesson was held up as exemplary.

This teacher was able to draw on her intellect and deliver 'learning' whilst also improvising in the moment with her deeper intelligence and trusting the insight that emerged. Once again, this is a great example of the intellect and insights weaving a dance of magic.

The intuitive intelligence of life that runs through Nature also runs through you.

The Inner Diamond is the place to look.

An insight is a form of seeing something afresh, without using the grind of your intellect. The most transformational insights are ones where you catch a glimpse of your True Nature. When you see through the mists of who you aren't to the truth of who you are then you feel a sense of freedom and creativity.

As a Wellbeing Listener you are creating a settled space which encourages the intellect to subside and enables your resilience and wellbeing to shine through.

This is a great space for insights.

Earlier in the chapter I shared the story of the students who were in the Wellbeing Group. They weren't taught techniques to think positively, they didn't learn concepts or memorise theories. These students were pointed in the direction of their Inner Diamond, to that source of resilience, wellbeing and True Nature. They all saw something afresh through insight.

Each insight they encountered was an insight into who they truly are, their True Self. They didn't need to think harder, smarter or faster, they just needed to trust themselves and to witness their inner pre-existing intelligence. The mental freedom and relief they encountered came through insights.

You Intuitively Know What's Needed

In my work as a coach (prior to coming across the Inside-Out understanding) I had a misunderstanding about insights. I often saw my clients accessing insights but back then I always assumed that when clients saw something fresh that it was somehow down to the coaching. I had built up a toolbox of ideas, concepts and techniques, so it made sense to me to attribute my success as a coach to these tools rather than to the natural emergence of insights from my clients.

Several years ago, before Wellbeing Listeners and the Inner Compass, I taught Coaching Skills. Back then I used the GROW model. I trained people in listening skills and I was convinced that the models and coaching tools were the things that made the difference in conversations.

My belief was that if you learn enough tools, theories and concepts you should be able to pull the right tool out of the toolbox for the client you are with.

There were two situations that started me questioning the power of tools and techniques.

The first was a situation when we were assessing some coaches who had been on our training. Part of the assessment was to watch them engage in a coaching conversation. To pass the assessment they had to show their use of the GROW model (it's a common coaching model to structure a conversation) and they had to illustrate good listening skills.

There were two contrasting coaching conversations.

The first was someone who had learnt the GROW model and was demonstrating his listening. The session felt artificial, it was more of a performance. Although on the face of it he displayed the skills, there was something missing. He scored highly because he was matching the criteria.

The second person was someone who dropped into a deep space of connection with her client. The session was sublime, the insights from the client were rich, but this coach didn't score highly.

The marking criteria we had for the assessment wasn't designed to give a good grade for this kind of connection.

This was the first situation where something felt amiss with the coaching skills we were teaching.

The second situation where I questioned the power of tools and techniques was in a primary school with a group of ten-year olds who we were training to become coaches. We were curious about what would happen if these ten-year-olds supported the younger children.

For three weeks we shared a child-friendly coaching model and then we introduced these coaches to their coachees (8-year-olds). I remember my dismay at the seeming bedlam that ensued. I imagined quiet conversations in the classroom, but the youngsters were playing, laughing and running around outside having games.

I was lucky to have a wise Classroom Assistant with me. She allowed this all to happen, whilst I wanted to bring everyone back in and to instil order.

I'm so glad I didn't interfere.

Two weeks later it dawned on me that these children were far more intuitive and far wiser than I ever imagined. Their coaching was more powerful and dynamic than anything I could come up with.

One of the coaches was Isabelle. She'd been paired up with a younger child, Mary, who was painfully shy. Mary turned up to the first session red eyed, she was so scared she wouldn't even whisper her name. Isabelle took the reluctant Mary into the playground for the coaching

When we gathered together after the coaching we sat once again on the carpet. This time Mary was smiling. As we asked the coachees what they had been up to, Mary raised her hand to speak. In a purposeful whisper she said, "Isabelle has been helping me find my voice."

I was stunned.

What had Isabelle done in the space of twenty minutes to facilitate this transformation from a teary, red-eyed, frightened mouse?

Isabelle later explained that she'd taken Mary into the playground with a netball and they'd played catch. Every time Mary caught the ball she had to say 'My name is Mary'. At first, they were side-by-side throwing the ball. Mary was whispering her name. By the end of the session, they were several metres apart and now Mary was shouting her name. Isabelle had intuitively done this without any prompting from us.

At the time I was baffled. How had Isabelle known what to do? Now I look back and it is obvious. Isabelle was in touch with her natural, deeper intelligence. She was in touch with her Inner Diamond and she listened to that. Insights flowed freely with Isabelle as she came up with ideas of how to support Mary.

Insights flowed freely with Mary as she started to see through the prison of her insecure thinking and to trust the natural flow of her resilience and wellbeing.

Back then I didn't understand the power of the Inner Diamond, or insights or the deeper intelligence behind life.

Looking back it is so powerful to see insights at work. It is so freeing to see what happens when children and adults get back in touch with their Inner Diamond.

It's such a relief to know that you are much more than you think you are.

The more you look in the direction of your Inner Diamond the more it makes sense to trust your natural, deeper, intuitive energy and to trust the insights that always arise.

Summary

- There is a big difference between what is natural and what is normal. It's likely you've confused the two.

- The world you are in has normalised stress. Living in sustained stress is not a healthy way to live, it is not natural.

- Nature is guided by a deeper, natural intuitive intelligence. You too are connected to this natural intelligence.

- When you see this natural intelligence, your Inner Diamond, you start to naturally align yourself with a more healthy, balanced way of living.

- Insights are commonplace and come from this deeper intuitive, natural wisdom. An insight is a kind of learning that by-passes the intellect. You haven't been trained to look for and trust insights.

- Insights are common and feel effortless. When you understand the power of insights you will cease to use your intellect in the same, overactive way.

FAQ
Does this mean I shouldn't plan – I should just wait for insight?

Of course you shouldn't sit around and do nothing, waiting for inspiration to strike.

Planning, considering the future and creating aspirations and goals are all part of the richness of the human experience.

I wouldn't be able to run a business, write a book or meet up with friends for coffee if I didn't use my intellect to help me organise my life.

It's also worth noting that I wouldn't be able to appreciate a beautiful sunset, laugh at the antics of my dog or feel gratitude at nature's generosity if it weren't for my natural intelligence.

There is a real richness in discovering the interconnected dance between the intellect and your deeper intelligence.

The intellect on its own is not the answer. The intellect can only take you part way.

I love how a high-wire artist described his art. He

needed his intellect to plan his diary, safely put up the wire and check the weather conditions.

When he was on the wire, he needed to be present and aware. His intellect was no longer the master, he was trusting his intuition. He knew that as soon as his mind wandered from taking the next step, he was at risk of falling. His whole attention was on being grounded and centred.

In your life you need both intellect and insight. You need your engaged mind and your deeper, intuitive intelligence.

I used to be a habitual planner and organiser. My love of planning spilt over into trying to get others to be organised. I liked things to be a certain way.

Now I see the value in both planning and allowing, in having a structure but also letting things flow.

A simple example of the difference is when we go for a day trip.

In the past I wanted to know where we were going, where we might stop for lunch, where we should walk and what time we needed to get back home. The trouble of living like this is that I was never fully present to anything.

Before we set out, I was imagining the car trip, on the car trip I was thinking about getting to our lunch venue on time, during lunch I was focussing on the walk and then on the walk I was imagining my trip home. If any of these things deviated from my plan, I felt a sense of panic.

I felt as though I was living a rushed life, always imagining the next thing that was going to happen, rather than being present.

Now I might plan a similar day trip, but I no longer treat it like a series of things to tick off my to-do list. The sense of urgency in my life has disappeared. If we're late for lunch, or the car breaks down or we choose to take a different walk, then I find myself curious about what's happening, rather than feeling a panic that I'm losing control.

It's not just day trips, this permeates my whole life. Our current Social Enterprise 'Inner Compass Guide CIC' has been an evolution and unfolding of events. I've allowed myself to be drawn to what is happening and I put energy and time to that which feels 'right' rather than spending copious time planning and trying to make things happen. This sense of something feeling 'right' is me listening beyond my intellect, noticing my Inner Compass pointing to my Inner Diamond and trusting my natural wisdom.

You don't need to make a choice between your intellect and deeper intelligence. It's a good idea to use both. If you haven't trusted your natural wisdom for a while, then it might take time to reconnect to what it feels like; trust me it will be worth it.

In Action:
When Laughter Replaces Family Dramas

Claire went on the Wellbeing Listener Programme to become a better listener. She realised she sometimes jumped in too quickly when listening to others.

Claire got much more from the programme than just listening skills. Claire started to notice her thoughts and feelings; she started to listen to herself.

The impact on her family was surprising.

She found that when her children erupted into a 'drama' of feelings, she didn't follow them, she was able to stand back and take a breath.

This was new for Claire. Usually, she responded in the same way and the family ended up in this drama of feelings.

Claire says that the family still has its stormy moments,

but she's also noticing the incredible laughter that seems to be spontaneously taking place in her house.

She feels a real optimism where once she felt 'downtrodden'.

Claire attributes this change of atmosphere in her house to her understanding of the Inner Diamond. She is quicker to notice when she feels out of kilter with her emotions. Claire notices a sense of calm that stretches beyond her; she says she is less likely to follow her unsettled thoughts and feelings.

Your Turn

Can you notice the difference between having insights and using the intellect to figure something out? Insights are easeful and gentle and seem to pop like bubbles of creativity in your mind. The intellect requires you to whirr up the cogs in your mind and to think and to try and find answers.

P.S.

I wonder what would happen if you didn't train the intellect and fan the flames of your mind in the way that you do? I wonder what would happen if you allowed the creative, innovative energy of life to freely be?

Chapter 6

Your Inner Compass Is Always Guiding You Home

"Teach only love, for that is what you are." *

Learning to Trust Your Inner Compass

We live on the edge of Dartmoor; it's a wild and expansive landscape. Rocky, granite outcrops are scattered across the moor, along with bogs and marshes. The moor is like a sponge and when the weather systems race off the Atlantic the rain falls, and the low clouds scud across the hills, shrouding the moors in a blanket of mist.

There are countless legends of the pixies and fairy-folk who lead unwary travellers astray. It's easy to believe those legends, especially when the mist descends. It's wise to keep to the well-worn paths when you're on the moors.

One day a mist came down and I decided to leave the moorland paths that I usually walk. I wanted to try out a compass and to see if I could find my way through the mist.

I had walked the hills countless times and I knew the terrain well. I was curious to see if I could trust an old-fashioned compass. This was a traditional compass and not a gadget on my smartphone.

I headed up onto the moors and into the fog.

When I stepped off the path and set out into the swirling mist my world became disorientating.

Within five minutes I lost my bearings.

---

* A Course in Miracles

I found it hard to discern if I was walking up or down hill. Trees and rocks loomed out of the mist; they seemed alien to me.

Where was I? Had I lost my way completely? My mind was racing; time seemed to have warped. I couldn't tell if I'd walked a mile or five miles.

This was when I took out my compass.

I knew the compass would point north and I knew I needed to travel south. I lined up the compass and took my bearings with something that was south of me. I could only see a few metres in front of me, so sometimes I lined up with a tree, or a gorse bush and sometimes it was a rock.

I walked a few steps to the object and then stopped and looked at the compass again and took my bearings off something else.

My mind continued to race with fears. *What if I got stuck? How would I get back? What if I strayed into a bog?*

I ignored these thoughts and continued to trust the compass.

It was a slow process of walking a few metres at a time. But I carried on until I found my way off the moor and back home.

I needed to try the compass for myself; I needed to know that I could trust it.

Having experienced that adventure in the mist, I now know I can deeply trust the compass if I get lost on the moors.

The compass only has one job. Its job is to point north. Even when I'm on unfamiliar territory, when the weather changes the compass will guide me home.

If you know you can rely on the compass, then you can work out the direction you need to take. A compass won't tell you what to do. It doesn't matter if you ignore it or forget to look at a compass, it will always point north.

Our Social Enterprise is called the Inner Compass Guide.

Pointing You Back to You

It seems to me that we all have an Inner Compass. Rather than pointing 'north' this Inner Compass points to our True Self, to our True Nature.

When you know you can trust the compass, then you know the direction to travel in.

The Wellbeing Listener journey is one that encourages you to trust your own compass. As you trust your Inner Compass then you know it will be with you in any situation or circumstance you find yourself in.

I know to trust that deeper, intuitive intelligence within me.

When I feel lost, I take it as a sign to seek out the ever-present sense of knowing and spaciousness.

When I feel anxious, or worried or overwhelmed, when the mist races and swirls in my mind, then I know that is a sign for me to seek out and trust my compass.

Those insecure feelings are useful. They provide good information. Those feelings let me know I am believing the stories of who I am not.

Those feelings are a reminder that peace-of-mind will never be found in the direction of those thoughts and feelings.

My Inner Compass always points in the same direction, it points toward my Inner Diamond.

It's good to know I can trust it.

If you have both a compass and a map that you can trust, then you will always find your way home.

If You're on Dartmoor a Map of Exmoor Won't Get You Home

When I was a child, I wondered why Australians didn't fall into space.

We had a globe at home; England was at the top of it and Australia was at the bottom.

I knew about gravity. When I dropped something, it fell to the floor. It always fell down and it never fell upwards.

To my childish mind if gravity was pulling everything downwards then the Australians should be pulled by gravity off the planet. I couldn't understand how they managed to stay on the earth. It was a complete mystery.

I can look back and smile at my childish misunderstanding, but at the time it baffled me.

When we only partially understand how something works, then we come to wrong conclusions.

It's the same with maps. If I am up on Dartmoor, but I'm reading a map of Exmoor, then I'll always be lost. There might be times when the landscape accidently lines up with the map in front of me. Maybe I spot a river, or a road that corresponds to one on the map. However, if I have the wrong map then, ultimately it is no good for the journey I'm undertaking.

I spent many years trying to make sense of my psychological world by reading the wrong map.

The map I had been following told me:

• I'm broken and I need fixing.
• I need to get rid of limiting beliefs.
• I need to work hard and work smarter to be a success.
• I need to get rid of anxiety, worry and insecurity.

I didn't realise it at the time, but I was following the wrong map.

Your Inner Compass and the Correct Map Gets You Home

Your Inner Compass is something you can trust.

The Wellbeing Listener journey provides you with a good map and it also helps you recognise that you have an internal navigation system to follow.

This book has been about finding the right map and helping you to read your compass.

We've covered many areas. All of these areas are designed to support you in orienting yourself with the right map. During this book you've also explored your deeper intelligence within; your Inner Diamond.

Let's take a moment to look at the landscape you've been through. There have been many markers, signposts and stopping places along the way.

As a Wellbeing Listener you've been learning about:

- Red and Green Thinking.
- The ups and downs of being human.
- The way that thought comes and goes.
- Your thoughts and feelings are like the weather, they are ever-changing.
- The sun is like your wellbeing, it is always shining.

As you've read this Wellbeing Listener book you've discovered:

- Your Inner Diamond of wellbeing.
- That at your core you are built of love and resilience.
- This core or essence is your True Nature; it is like the sun.
- You can become distracted by the fearful thoughts that get in your way.
- Like clouds blocking the sun, thoughts can obscure your True Nature, but not damage it.

On this Wellbeing journey you've seen that:

- The outside world can't make you feel anything.
- Your thoughts and feelings dictate how you see the world.
- Your thoughts and feelings are not who you really are.
- There is a natural source of intelligence you can tap into.

- Insights are the agent of transformation.
- There is a big difference between what's natural and what's normal.

As you've explored being a listener you'll know:

- It's important to listen to yourself before listening to others.
- It's powerful to listen deeply to others.
- There's no answer in the story.
- People don't want fixing or solutions, they want to be heard.
- Listening helps people to access Green Thinking (your intuitive, insightful thinking).

 Isn't it good to see this rich and varied trek you've been on? When you see all the landmarks along the way, it might look like a lot to take in and digest. However, it's very simple. Just remember two things - the map and the compass:

- The map reminds you that your thoughts and feelings come and go, they aren't who you are.
- Your Compass points to your True Nature. At your core you are resilience and wellbeing; you can't be broken.

A Clear Sign You're Misreading the Map

I was out walking on Dartmoor and I suddenly noticed my head was quiet. I stopped beside a gushing stream. Heavy rain had washed the water crystal clear and deep pools enticed Buzz the labradoodle in for a swim.

Here on the moor with the bracken turning orange with autumn, I was alone; there were no cars, no houses and no people. I stood still and closed my eyes. Other than the breeze brushing against my ear and the occasional skylark, there was silence. I breathed deeply, feeling a well of gratitude rise within.

What a contrast to how I felt just a few days earlier.

At the beginning of the week I'd returned from a recent holiday. I'd been fighting a brain that was reluctant to return to work, I had been rushing around writing emails, catching up with clients and feeling a sense of being overwhelmed. Whispering worries cluttered my mind. Feelings of insecurity, doubt and guilt took turns at trying to get my attention.

- *"You're not cut out for work – you're too old."*
- *"You're a bad daughter for not seeing your parents whilst on holiday."*
- *"You're hopeless at keeping on top of work."*

Wave after wave of insecurities washed on the shore of my mind and a sense of urgency gripped me. I wanted to rid myself of these uncomfortable feelings.

It appeared to me that I needed to sort many things out in my life. I needed to get more organised, see my parents more often, be a better trainer, not go on holiday again, write more emails … and so the list went on.

In the past I would have become busy trying to fix all these agitated thoughts and feelings. In the past I would have tried harder and worked faster. To me it would look like these feelings were telling me about my incompetence, my inability to be professional, my lack of empathy as a daughter and my failure as a coach and trainer.

In reality those thoughts were only telling me one thing: that I was lost in insecure thinking at that moment.

The beauty of understanding insecure thinking is that I know that all of these feelings and related stories about my incompetence, are only ever telling me one thing. It is the same for you.

Whenever you feel unsettled then your Inner Compass

is letting you know that you're misreading your 'map'. You know you're misreading your map if you're looking for that relief, deeper connection or a sense of feeling settled from the outside world or by controlling circumstances. It doesn't matter what story you're telling yourself or what feeling or thought you're experiencing. Your Inner Compass is reminding you that there is only one place to look for peace-of-mind and ease, and that is to look within.

When I feel anxious or insecure then I know I'm looking for peace-of-mind in the wrong direction. These unsettled feelings are a reminder to look towards my deeper, intuitive space of wisdom and awareness. This space of awareness is always present no matter what is happening to me.

As I stood beside the Dartmoor stream and breathed in deeply once again, I felt myself on firm ground. It had taken several days for my mind to settle and for the stories to subside, but I hadn't got lost by reading the wrong map. I hadn't started to chase happiness, I had known, at a deeper level, that I needed to stop analysing the thoughts in my head and to keep looking to the space within.

There is a real sense of liberation in realising there is only ever one place to look. My only purpose in life is to keep being curious about my inner sense of awareness, to give attention to the place that feels like 'home' within.

When I trust this foundational intuitive wisdom then I see life as an unfolding miracle and not as a constant battle that needs to be fought.

Tree by Tree You Will See the Whole Landscape

As you reach the end of the book it might seem as though you're at the end of your Wellbeing Listener journey. If you look back at the terrain you've been through, you'll notice many landmarks along the way. But are you

actually at the end of the journey? As a Wellbeing Listener the learning has only just begun.

Ugborough Beacon is the hill above our house and from the top you can see for miles. It's on the edge of Dartmoor and if you look north you can see the empty and wild moors.

In contrast, if you turn southwards you can see rich and fertile farmlands. A collage of misshapen, rectangular fields and farms, and the occasional town or village heading towards the coast. Ten to twelve miles away is the sea and when the sun is shining the water can glow, like liquid gold.

I love walking up to the top of Ugborough Beacon and soaking up the view, it's a stunning landscape.

If I take a visitor to the top of The Beacon, I point out different towns and villages in the southern view. But with such an open vista, at first it can be hard to make things out. It's helpful to 'lead' their eye in the right direction.

First, I point to something close to us, like a tree and once my friend has spotted the tree I ask them to look further off, maybe towards a distinguishing house, or mast and then eventually, step-by-step I take their eye to the town I want them to spot.

This gentle, slow way of pointing out towns in a wide-open landscape, is a bit like the Wellbeing Listener journey.

We're pointing out landmarks along the way, encouraging you to see further and further in the right direction. It's a slow and gradual experience.

The journey of the Wellbeing Listener is one to help you understand how you operate as a human being on a psychological level. In this instance, when we talk of psychology, we are using the original meaning of psychology. This is the study (ology) of the soul (psych). If you continue the exploration of 'soul study' then you'll discover that this is a rich and varied journey.

Why the Strange Tree Isn't the End, It's Just the Beginning

This book isn't the end, instead, see it as a stepping-stone to a whole new experience of life. This book is pointing out the first part of the journey, there is much more to see.

When I talk about Red and Green Thinking, imagine you are on top of Ugborough Beacon. I want to show you a village in the distance and to help you spot it, I'm pointing to a rock a few metres away to help you line up your eye. With the Red and Green Thinking we're not describing a destination, or a concept. We're offering Red and Green Thinking as a metaphor; we're inviting you to consider that the world works in a different way than you originally thought.

Red and Green Thinking is the equivalent of me and you on top of Ugborough Beacon and me pointing out the rock that is just ahead of us. The rock is a way to line up your eyesight with the village that is several miles distant. We both know the rock isn't the end point, it is just the beginning.

Don't be fooled into thinking that by understanding Red and Green Thinking you're now going to be suddenly 'better'.

The 'rock' is not the destination, it is the direction of travel.

It's the same with the Inner Diamond.

As we look beyond the rock, I point out a strange looking tree on the hillside a mile away. The Inner Diamond is that strange looking tree. The Inner Diamond is just a metaphor and it is the next place to align your eyes. It is the next landmark beyond the rock that I've pointed out in the foreground.

If you fixate on the 'strange tree' then you can start to ponder on the Inner Diamond.

At first it looks like the Inner Diamond is personal. It is all about you having an Inner Diamond and me having an Inner Diamond. It looks like we are all walking around with internal (metaphorical) diamonds. But that's not ultimately what I'm hoping you'll get to see.

Keep looking … keep looking beyond the strange tree. Further in the distance your eyes will alight on a distinctive building and you'll realise that the Inner Diamond is not telling you about your individual resilience and wellbeing. The Inner Diamond is actually a description of the universal energy that is behind life.

Your Inner Diamond is a metaphor for the spiritual awareness from which you are able to have the experience of being alive. The source of all of us is from this ever-present, loving, compassionate energy and that is why you are ultimately OK, at your core you are made of wellbeing and resilience.

As you move through this landscape from the rock to the tree to the building, you start to see new landmarks on the horizon. You realise that at each stage of your journey there is more to see. Of course, we're not actually talking about a physical journey, we're not talking about fixating on things in the outside world. The landscape you're navigating is one within you.

If you're anything like me you've spent a lifetime trying to fix your personality, thoughts and feelings. I've spent an age trying to be a better person. I've also wanted other people to change their ways.

However, unlike the frantic, revved up thinking that you're used to engaging in, the journey of the Wellbeing Listener is different. This is a nourishing, rich exploration.

The more you explore, the simpler you realise it actually is. You realise you no longer need to rid yourself of negative thoughts and you see that each mood and feeling is welcome because it isn't who you truly are. You'll also understand that you aren't broken and that whilst you might become lost you have an Inner Compass to point you back to your True Nature. As you realise all these things for yourself then you can also be a great support to others.

Isn't it good to see that there is much more to experience and learn? Isn't it a relief to see that you can't be broken? Isn't it good to know that when you listen to yourself, to your True Nature, you are of best possible service to others?

To Listen is to Love

The world is full of people who are mentally exhausted, they're striving and working towards a better future. What they fail to realise is that the essence of who they are is actually within. They fail to realise that the very thing they're looking for (love, resilience, resourcefulness, peace-of-mind) is actually who they truly are.

It only takes a shift of focus to realise this.

Your Inner Compass is pointing you away from your thoughts, emotions and moods towards your deeper knowing.

As you start to take your attention away from your personal identity and instead look inwards towards the ever-present awareness, then you are starting to experience the true magic, mystery and wonder of life itself.

We hope you will continue this rich exploration and continue to see that what you seek (love, peace and compassion) is who you truly are.

As you experience love, peace and compassion in yourself, so you realise that love, peace and compassion is present in everyone.

Listening for wellbeing is listening out for that love, peace and resilience in others. It is what you naturally do when you realise that the true power lies in people realising that they are actually deeply OK, they aren't broken, and they don't need fixing.

The act of listening is an act of love. It is a catalyst that helps you to remember who you truly are. As you listen out for your Inner Diamond, and you listen to my Inner Diamond, then we find ourselves connecting at an energetic level that is beyond concepts, ideas and personalities.

The world is full of people who are thirsty to be heard. They want to be heard at the level of the soul. As a Wellbeing Listener we encourage you to be those ears for others and to let others realise the true potential and power that is their birth right. Listening is a gift; it is your gift to the world.

As a Wellbeing Listener you aren't responsible for the other person to feel better, or to have insights or to be happy. Your only responsibility is to listen out for their Inner Diamond and to point them in that direction. What they see (or don't see) isn't on you.

Stu (my husband) and I have an aspiration that communities can be founded on Wellbeing Listening. The mental agitation and noise that distracts and drains us, can leave people isolated, depressed and tired.

What would it be like to live in a world where we listen out to connect rather than fix? What if we listen out to experience love, rather than seek approval and if we listen to express our oneness rather than our separation? What if we are listening from a space of love?

Listening is ordinary, natural and a balm for the soul. In our local community of Ivybridge we're sharing this simple way of listening. Wellbeing Listeners are coming together to offer mutual support and to create pockets of connection in the community. I describe more about this in the 'How to Become a Wellbeing Listener' section at the end of the book.

We would love you to join our Wellbeing Listening (r)evolution. You can join us online and meet with other like-minded people who are taking small steps to make the world a better place. We would love you to experience the joy, gratitude and nourishment that arises from realising that listening is an act of love.

Summary

- Get a feel for your 'Inner Compass'. This is your intuitive guidance system that will point you back towards your space of creativity, resilience and resourcefulness.

- When you understand how your thinking works then you have the right 'map'. Your thinking shifts and changes. Your unsettled thinking lets you know you're misreading the map.

- Whatever unsettled and insecure thinking you feel, it is only letting you know one thing. It is letting you know you are looking for peace-of-mind in the wrong direction. Turn your attention within.

- This is the start of a long, nourishing and rich exploration. If you've started to see things shift for you, then keep being curious. There's lots more to see.

- Listening is an act of love. As you listen in to your Inner Diamond you'll notice the Inner Diamond of others. From that space you will experience a deep connection.

FAQs

Is giving advice 'bad'?

I always recommend that you pause before giving advice to someone. When someone comes to you in agitated thinking, then it's understandable that you want to help ease their angst. Often it seems that giving advice is the answer to their unsettled thinking.

There is nothing wrong with giving advice. It is not intrinsically bad. The setback of giving advice is that it usually isn't needed.

I love this quote from Michael Neill. He sums it up so well:

"The problem with advice, or so I've always thought, is that when you most feel like you need it you're usually in no state to follow it; when you're up for following it, you usually don't need it."

As a Wellbeing Listener we're encouraging you to understand the power of listening to another person so that their mind settles. What you'll invariably find, is that when someone has a settled mind then they find the answer they need.

It's tempting to believe that giving someone an answer will create a settled mind. The opposite is true. When someone's mind settles then the answer appears.

I remember coaching a 15-year-old lad who was disorganised. Every day he turned up at school without a pen, without the right books and without his completed homework. His teachers were at their wits end.

As the lad told me about the chaotic start to his day, I felt real empathy. He was a carer for his mum and had lots of things to consider before making his way to school. Whilst he was talking, the 'obvious' answer popped into my mind. If this lad were to pack his bags the night before then his problems of rushing around in the morning would be solved.

As a Wellbeing Listener, I paused before giving him the 'answer' to his problem. He had a lot on his plate and I first wanted to hear what his life was like. As the conversation quietened down, I suppressed my desire to 'give' him the answer (pack your bags the night before) and instead sat with him.

"I need to be more organised," he said thoughtfully.

I instinctively knew that many people in his life would have given advice on how to be organised and I didn't want to add to the nagging voices in his head. I could also tell he was troubled that he found things so overwhelming. I felt for him and I felt connected.

Then suddenly a question popped into my head. "Who do you know who is organised?" He paused before answering and then with half a smile he said, "The girls are more organised." He went on to explain that they came to school with the right books, the right homework and a pen.

"I wonder what the girls are doing?" I asked curiously. The question hung in the air as he turned it over in his mind. Then his eyes lit up, he'd had an insight.

"The girls pack their bags the night before," he said this with an edge of wonder in his voice. He'd seen something afresh.

We then carried on the conversation and he started to explore how he might do the same thing in his life. From that day onwards, he always packed his bag the night before. It made absolute sense to him, so that's what he did.

The point of telling you this story about the young lad is that the 'advice' I might have given him at the start of the conversation to pack his bags the night before, wouldn't have been heard.

People don't hear 'advice' when their head is busy and full. It doesn't matter how good that advice or solution is, if someone can't hear it then they won't take it on.

When you instead listen, you give space and you allow someone's thinking to settle, then from a clear head the 'advice' they need will occur to them.

Have you noticed that it is much more powerful when you work out your own solution, rather than trying to adopt someone else's idea?

The first role of a Wellbeing Listener is to listen. Keep listening and you'll see how listening is the catalyst for the mind to settle. If you've created a space for someone to experience a settled mind, then you've done your job well. It

is from the space of a settled mind that someone is likely to find the right way forward and from this settled mind they'll feel resourced and resilient in taking the next step.

In Action: The Case of Ordinary Magic

In 2021 I started a Community Hub with Jessica, the Ivybridge Community Connector and a fellow Wellbeing Listener.

We were inspired (post Covid-19 lockdowns) to create a space for the community to have a free cup of tea, to learn about clubs, groups and activities in the town and to have a go at something new.

The pilot was a great success and a group of residents joined us and tried out art, relaxations, aromatherapy, origami and table tennis.

Alice was one of the people who turned up for our table-tennis session. During the morning we transformed the room. There were three tiny improvised 'table-tennis' tables and people having a go at knocking a ball across the net.

After the activity we sat down for a cup of tea; we fell into a conversation and laughed about the table tennis antics. In our conversation, like the ping pong ball, we chatted to and fro. This is an ordinary, everyday, interaction.

As a Wellbeing Listener I was shining a light on the fun and connection of the experience. At the end of the conversation Alice turned to me and said a heart-felt 'Thank you'.

Alice went on to explain that she had felt really flat and low when she arrived. "I had a lot on my mind," she explained. Alice then went on to say how she felt lighter, how she no longer felt low or down. "Being out this morning has done me the world of good."

What Alice was experiencing was a sense of her own wellbeing in the moment. To her it might have looked like the table-tennis was the reason behind her feeling better. However, it wasn't the table-tennis that made her feel better. As she took her attention away from the stormy thinking of her mind, her thoughts (Red Thinking) naturally settled.

In the absence of Red Thinking, she naturally experienced her own Inner Diamond shining through. She was having a taste of her own built-in resilience and wellbeing.

Alice was a recipient of Wellbeing Listening. In this instance it turned up as a natural, light-hearted, connected interaction that reminded her that she has resilience, wellbeing and resourcefulness built into her psychological system.

P.S.

There is a beautiful simplicity in seeing the exquisite ordinariness of life. The more you trust the deeper energy of life (Inner Diamond) the clearer and freer your mind becomes. The more you trust your Inner Compass the more you will navigate with joy, gratitude and ease through life. What more could you want?

TO LISTEN IS TO LOVE

What Are the 'Three Principles'?

When I came across the Three Principles my life changed completely. It was like coming to a fork in the road and choosing a path that took me on an unexpected nourishing journey; it opened my eyes in a way I never imagined possible.

Since exploring this path, nothing has fundamentally changed in my life, and yet, at the same time everything seems different. I'm still happily married, I'm still a coach, I still run my business and I still have a great family. The biggest difference for me is the whirring noise and whispering doubts that used to follow me around no longer take centre stage.

My head is quieter, and life is now much more easeful.

I have so much to thank the Three Principles (3Ps) for, however we rarely refer to the 3Ps in our training nowadays. We have found a language and way of describing things that works for us. The 3Ps still inform our work, but we use the term 'Inside-Out' and the metaphors of the 'Inner-Compass' and 'Inner Diamond' to communicate our ideas.

Let me give you a potted history of the 3Ps.

The Three Principles were first articulated by Sydney Banks. He was a Scottish welder who had an enlightenment experience. This experience came out of the blue. He went from being an incredibly insecure man to having absolute mental freedom. Syd had a first-hand experience of the awareness behind life itself. He spent several years trying to find words for what he'd seen, and people came from all over the world to visit this 'enlightened man' who lived on Salt Spring Island in Canada.

Over time Syd began to find it helpful to describe what he'd seen through the metaphor of the Three Principles. These principles point to the fundamental and unchanging understanding of what it is to be human. Syd died in 2009 and the legacy of his work has been carried on by other teachers.

The principles are:

Mind – which refers to the life-energy behind everything.
Thought – the shifting energy that creates our experience of life.
Consciousness – the awareness that brings thought to life.

I first heard of The Three Principles in 2012 – three years after Syd's death. In the early days I imagined Syd Banks was a shiny-white-toothed American with jet black hair, a booming voice and a slick stage presence. When I first saw a video of him, I laughed. I wasn't expecting a bearded, old, Scotsman sitting in an armchair!

Why we don't share the Three Principles

Over the years I've listened to and read and spoken to many people involved in the Three Principles community.

There are many great teachers of the Three Principles and I list some of the ones I've come across below. Many of these teachers directly learned from Syd Banks. I love hearing them speak. They have an aura of calm groundedness and a deeply authentic way of sharing what they see.

At first, I wanted to be like these great teachers. I tried to tell people about the Three Principles. The trouble was that my efforts were often confusing, and people seemed to get intellectually tangled in what I was trying to say. As a trainer when I referred to the 'Three Principles' people wanted to know what they were. When I tried to explain the

Three Principles, they became a concept which got in the way of real understanding.

Rather than talk about the Three Principles, Stu and I refer to the Inside-Out understanding. For us this is a short-hand way of saying 'look within'.

We've been lucky enough to visit the Three Principles School on Salt Spring Island. We've been on retreats with Dicken Bettinger, Keith Blevens, Ian Watson and Clare Brown, and Elsie Spittle (and we've run a retreat with Elsie). We've had training with Ken Manning and Robin Charbit, we've attended the Three Principles conference in the UK and spoken at events in Prague and in Spain, and we've run Three Principles Conferences in Devon. Stu and I have (between us) been on courses with Michael Neill and Jamie Smart.

More recently we've been intrigued by Non-Duality and have worked with Garret Kramer and been on retreats with Rupert Spira.

We've also interviewed many people for our podcasts including Ian Watson, Elizabeth Lovius, Dicken Bettinger, Sandy Krott, Natasha Swerdloff, Jamie Smart, Sam Jarman, Nicola Bird, Clare Dimond and many others.

Everything we've been involved in has been a beautiful stepping-stone for us to find our own language and articulation of what the Inside-Out (Three Principles) is pointing to.

Stu and I talk about 'The Inner Compass' which is our metaphor to describe the built-in navigation system. We find that this is a simple way of conveying that sense of 'knowing' and 'awareness' within.

When I first came across the Three Principles, I found it very hard to describe what they were. I avidly read, watched and listened to a lot of material. There are thousands of hours of free podcasts, videos and articles you can engage with. I know it can be overwhelming to sift through the enormous amount of material you can find online. So, I've done a bit of sifting for you and have chosen a small selection of authors, trainers and resources that spoke deeply to me. There are many more but try these for starters.

A Small Selection of Resources chosen by Liz

Sydney Banks: I strongly encourage you to read or listen to Sydney Banks Sydneybanks.org

If you search for him online, you'll find talks and interviews. He's written many books. My personal favourite is:

The Missing Link – Sydney Banks

Jamie Smart: Jamie is inspired by supporting coaches in developing thriving businesses. I went through Clarity Coach Training. He's a great trainer and speaker and has supported us on various conferences we've run. He is often on social media and provides lots of information, opportunities for coaching and tips. He's a Sunday Times Bestselling author. My personal favourite book is:

The Little Book of Clarity – Jamie Smart

Michael Neill: Michael Neill is a prolific blogger and has lots of podcasts, interviews and snippets from his training freely available online. Stu and I have both attended his training programmes.

My favourite book of his is:

The Inside-Out Revolution – Michael Neill

Jack Pransky: Jack is one of the people who learned directly from Syd Banks. He has a particular interest in community work. Jack has written many books about the 3Ps. There are two I want to recommend.

Modello: A Story of Hope for the Inner City: This is totally inspiring if you'd like to learn how this understanding can impact communities. This book is one I keep returning to.

Somebody Should Have Told Us!: This was one of the first books I read. Simple, clear and easy to read.

Elsie Spittle: Elsie knew Syd before his enlightenment experience. Many of his friends fell away after this experience but Elsie was one of the few friends to stay with him. She lives on Salt Spring Island. Elsie is a source of wonderful tales of Syd Banks. She is a great storyteller and brings to life the early years of working with Syd and sharing the Three Principles.

Elsie has written several books. I really enjoyed:

Our True Identity - Elsie Spittle

Linda Quiring: Linda Quiring was one of the first people to learn from Syd after his enlightenment experience. She leads a quiet life on Salt Spring Island. Her books *Island of Knowledge* and *Beyond Beliefs* are collaborations with Syd Banks. I love the book *Encounters with an Enlightened Man*. In it she shares what it was like with Syd just after his enlightenment experience and before he started sharing the Three Principles publicly.

Charbit, Manning and Krott. Robin Charbit, Ken Manning and Sandy Krott work extensively with big businesses, sharing the Three Principles in a way that can make huge differences to organisations dealing with issues and problems. They also train people who want to share this work in businesses. Their book *Invisible Power* is really comprehensive and easy to read. I often recommend this to my coaching clients.

Rupert Spira: Rupert Spira is not aligned with the 3Ps, but he's someone that Stu and I often listen to online. If you're interested in non-duality then take a look on YouTube and search for 'Rupert Spira'.

Podcasts: Please check out our podcasts and blogs at: innercompassguide.com/articles

If you'd like to sign up to our Newsletter, then you can do so on our website **www.innercompassguide.com**

I hope you enjoy exploring the Three Principles and Inside - Out understanding. Please get hold of me at: **liz@innercompassguide.com** if you'd like to connect.

How to Become a Wellbeing Listener

Here on the edge of Dartmoor in Ivybridge a listening revolution is taking root. In a world that can sometimes seem fractured and polarised, this promise of listening is a balm to those who long to be heard.

This listening revolution is low-key and gentle – maybe it's more of an evolution than revolution. It is like the soft rain that brushes my face after weeks of dry weather, or the gentle gurgling of the stream running over rocks.

Wellbeing Listening is the most simple and precious gift you can give to anyone. As you listen beyond the stories and fears then you start to hear the refreshing space of connection, compassion and love.

Humans are a beautifully diverse bunch and sometimes our differences can feel frightening and unsettling. In a world driven by social media and an overload of information, those messages of difference can be intensified.

The role of a Wellbeing Listener is to amplify the space of connection rather than separation. It is a way of enabling you to realise that the heart, soul and core of who you are, is the same as the heart, soul and core of me, and of us all.

As you shine a light on who you truly are, then you realise your fears around separation are not to be believed. Instead of feeling scared you are able to relish the differences and hear from those who hold other opinions.

Wellbeing Listening is the most simple, unobtrusive gift in the world.

If you've enjoyed this book and you'd like to learn more about becoming a Wellbeing Listener then take a look at our website **www.innercompassguide.com**

We recommend three steps:

1) First of all, attend one of our free Wellbeing Listener Zoom introductions. Email me to find out the dates: **liz@innercompassguide.com**

2) Join our month-long Wellbeing Listener Foundation. This programme has four sessions (each one and a half hours long) and two mentoring sessions. We run these both on Zoom and in person.

3) Become a Community Listener and explore Wellbeing Listening in your community. The Community Listener 6-month programme is an enriching space to deepen your understanding.

If you're curious about starting a Wellbeing Listening Community in your own town or village, and would like to follow our blue-print then check our website. The blue-print is an overview of how we have explored wellbeing in the community of Ivybridge. You can discover more at **innercompassguide.com.** That's also the place to visit if you would like to sign up to our regular email-blog.

You can join one of our online programmes or listen to our podcasts and blogs at **innercompassguide.com/articles**. Our Wellbeing Listener Introduction is free and it's a great way to join in the conversation.

In 2020 I stopped engaging on Social Media, my internal guidance system (my Inner Compass) pointed me away from it. I'm always keen to connect, so if you'd like to let me know what you think of this book please feel free to email me at **liz@innercompassguide.com.**

Acknowledgements

When people ask me how long it took to write this book I pause before answering. On the one hand it took 18 months and on the other hand it took 30 years. It seems as if I've been writing books and different drafts of books forever.

The difference with this book was finding Dorothy Kolomeisky. Dorothy's a writing coach and general inspirational genius who waved her magic wand whenever the writing gremlins set in. Whenever I faltered, Dorothy was there with her bright and breezy energy, nursing the creative goddess within. There is no doubt that Dorothy helped this book make it over the finishing line.

Then there's my husband Stu. Over the years, whenever I declared my intention to 'write a book' he has always unstintingly encouraged me. There are dozens of half written manuscripts saved on computers or clipped into binders. Stu has been behind each one, waving the flag and cheering me on. Stu is also co-founder of Inner Compass Guide CIC and we are co-facilitators on the Wellbeing Listener training. The material in this book originated from the Wellbeing Listener course that we created and designed together. Thankyou Stu.

Thanks mum. You've always pressed me to write a book. This might not be the best-selling work of fiction that you hoped I'd write, but it is a book. I hope you enjoy reading it.

I also want to thank my dear dad, whose dementia has robbed him of even recognising me (let alone realising I've written a book). In my younger days he kept urging me to write … if I had a time machine I'd love to let him know the book did see the light of day.

Then there's Erica Lewis. Erica was the coaching friend who first told me about the Three Principles. Without doubt, the 3Ps has been the most transformational influence on my work and life. Thanks for pointing me in the right direction Erica.

My sister Rachel has read so much of my material, blogs and articles over the years. It's very useful having an English teacher in the family. You are the best of sisters and I appreciate your feedback, love and support.

Thanks to all my dear friends and Wellbeing Listeners who read the final draft and kindly gave feedback and comments. Thanks also to Caroline Brewer and Ann Buckingham, they are Directors of Inner Compass Guide CIC and good friends as well.

Then of course I want to thank Becky Hawkins the illustrator. Becky is my old school friend. I've always been in awe of her artistic ability. I knew from day one that my gifted, artistic friend would be the person to illustrate the book. Thanks Becky for bringing this book to life.

Liz Scott is a Wellbeing Coach living on the edge of Dartmoor. After leaving the BBC in 2007 she started her own coaching business, working extensively with leaders in organisations and schools. In 2020 Liz and her husband Stu, created the social enterprise 'Inner Compass Guide CIC' to focus on their local community of Ivybridge. They run courses on Wellbeing Listening and collaborate across the town with community groups and businesses. Their vision is for everyone to live fulfilled and connected lives in their community. Their mission is to celebrate and acknowledge the natural resilience of the human spirit.